Finally!

To
Leslie,

Thank you and God bless!

Anthony Pi...

HOW TO STOP DATING LOSERS FOREVER

YOUR GUIDE TO GETTING THE MAN OF YOUR DREAMS

ANTHONY RICHE, PhD

iUniverse, Inc.
New York Lincoln Shanghai

Finally!
HOW TO STOP DATING LOSERS FOREVER

iUniverse books may be ordered through booksellers or by contacting:

iUniverse
2021 Pine Lake Road, Suite 100
Lincoln, NE 68512
www.iuniverse.com
1-800-Authors (1-800-288-4677)

The views expressed in this work are solely those of the author and do not necessarily reflect the views of the publisher, and the publisher hereby disclaims any responsibility for them.

ISBN-13: 978-0-595-41418-5 (pbk)
ISBN-13: 978-0-595-88389-9 (cloth)
ISBN-13: 978-0-595-85770-8 (ebk)
ISBN-10: 0-595-41418-4 (pbk)
ISBN-10: 0-595-88389-3 (cloth)
ISBN-10: 0-595-85770-1 (ebk)

Printed in the United States of America

CONTENTS

INTRODUCTION

Dating isn't an easy thing to do by any stretch of the imagination. There are no high school or college courses to teach or prepare us for the rigors of dating. We can watch all of the Hollywood movies we want, yet never come close to duplicating the romance and passion we see on the big screen. The reality is that dating is a skill, just like driving, playing sports or applying the right amount of makeup. Okay, maybe dating is *a little* harder than that, but it is a skill, nonetheless, and it's possible to learn how to become better at dating.

Living in New York City, I see a lot of people on a daily basis: in the streets, on the subway, in any one of the city's fifteen thousand restaurants. And I pay close attention to the couples I spot on the streets. I like to look at their body language and how they communicate with each other. I try to read the energy that forms around them, which gives me clues about the status of their relationship. It's fairly easy to tell who's happy and who's not.

I am amazed by the amount of women who appear to "settle" in their choices for a mate. I'll notice a guy being a complete ass around his girlfriend, and I'll wonder why she puts up with such behavior. Now, I may not know what goes on behind closed doors, but there are times when I see a couple, and I have to ask myself, "What does she see in him?" There is a science behind opposites attracting (Swiss psychologist, Dr. Carl Jung called extraversion and introversion), but there can be times when the opposites are just too opposite, like one person having a job while the other stays home to watch *Jerry Springer*. Or one person acting with class while the other acts like he's been raised on a pig farm.

It's moments like these when I wonder why women date losers. This is not to say that women can't be losers, too, but it seems like guys do a better job at pairing themselves up with exactly the type of mate they are looking for. Men seem to get what they want in a mate while women seem to settle. I wondered whether what I had noticed was just a numbers thing or if it was a sign of something deeper.

Then I thought of one of my best friends, a woman who is successful, attractive, and independent without being too independent. She is ambitious but also romantic. She is kind and caring and can't seem to find a decent guy to date. In fact, she seems to go from one loser to another. She knows so much about losers firsthand, she could've co-written this book with me. I've been there for her many late nights while she recounted her horror stories to me, and I always ask her, "Why do you always seem to date losers?" This wasn't a question that she hadn't already asked herself; it was a question for which she had no answer.

This question served as my inspiration for writing this book. I know there are scores of women out there, just like my friend, who either unconsciously attract losers or just seem to end up with them. In my work as a life coach and clinical hypnotherapist, I often see clients who are unhappy with their relationships. I believe that if people in general, and women in particular, knew how to make better choices in the area of picking and choosing a mate they would increase their chances of being happy overall and feeling more successful in general. Being in a relationship doesn't exclusively define who we are as people. but it's an important aspect of our lives. Life is all about choices. The choices you make affect the outcome of your life. Unfortunately, not all of us have been taught how to make good choices, and many times we emulate the choices we saw while growing up. Other times, we make the conscious decision *not* to make the same choices we saw while growing up. Either way, using these principles means you are operating from a weakened position. You are trying to tweak a model that you've found before you instead of *creating your own* model.

Within this book, you'll find tips on how to make better choices from a position of power——not one dictated by the past, but one based on your future. You will be able to identify why you attract losers and what you can do about it. Throughout this book, there will be short quizzes and anecdotes that will sharpen your skill and increase your knowledge in dating the right man for you. It is my hope that by the end of this book, you will have all of the insight and confidence you need to go out and find the mate you deserve. You should be able to find someone who is going to love and respect you and make you feel appreciated without having to play any mind games. There are good, healthy relationships out there; you just have to know how to choose them.

CHAPTER ONE

ARE YOU A LOSER MAGNET?

Has this ever happened to you? You're out on a hot date with a guy you recently met. You sit down, and, after placing your order with the waiter, you begin the customary getting-to-know-you conversation. Within only ten minutes of the conversation, you're ready to bolt. You can't believe some of the things that are coming out of this man's mouth. Then you think, "No wonder this guy is single!"

It's another date with another dud. You're disappointed, and soon you begin to wonder, "What's wrong with me?" Once you're past that stage, it's on to: "All the good guys are taken, and there's nothing left but losers." This may seem like a fact, but it's not. There really are plenty of good guys out there just as there are plenty of losers out there. The problem with your dating life could be that you've been attracting the wrong types of guys, and that's what's keeping you in a frustrating cycle of *loser dating*. Date enough losers, and it can begin to affect your self-esteem (not to mention kill what little hope you may have left in mankind). Yes, some guys can be real jerks, but there are also some guys out there who are loving and caring. A guy may not be perfect, because perfection just doesn't exist, but his minor flaws won't outweigh his positives.

So if you're ready to find a good guy, the first step is to identify who the bad guys are. Let's take a closer look.

What Is a Loser?

A loser is a guy who has major flaws in his personality that translate into his personal life. This guy really needs to do some work on himself, but he is either too frightened to make such changes or is downright adamant about not needing to change. His personality flaws serve him and only him, so asking him to change for you or anyone else sounds to him like a foolish proposition. He just doesn't

1

want to hear it. What he gets from being the way he is far outweighs what he'd be getting for giving up such behavior. He's aware of his flaws because he's heard about them many times before from other people, but he either hasn't made the effort to change or doesn't feel like he really has to.

This guy's been able to get away with such rudimentary behavior by finding people (i.e., *you*) who are willing to put up with his crap. And when each person becomes tired of his crap, he's onto the next willing participant. He won't change unless he *really* has to, either due to some life-changing experience, a major revelation, or intervention.

There are two levels of loserdom. There's what I like to call a Level I loser. This is the kind of guy that every sane girl should stay away from. He is damaging emotionally and can be very toxic to you. This guy needs serious help. And if you're looking for a reason behind why he is the way he is, let me save you the trouble and the heartache. It's all summed up in one word: *insecure.*

Then there's the Level II loser. He isn't as harmful as the Level I guy. He could even be cute … to someone else. This guy is really nothing but a big waste of time. If you like being stuck in one place with no growth, then this guy's for you. He's like your typical soap opera, you can tune in four years from now and his storyline still will not have changed.

Characteristics of a Loser

Next, I'll describe the characteristics of several different types of Level I losers. This level of loser is the most prevalent and dangerous; avoid them at all cost.

The Liar

The Liar is the loser that can cause you the most harm emotionally by destroying your ability to trust someone fully and completely. He can be very convincing and, chances are, very good at lying. His lies can be simple ones such as claiming he keeps a summer home in the Hamptons and has a Porsche that's in the shop. Or they can be big lies such as saying he's single when his wife is at home watching his three kids. He might work hard to convince you that he doesn't have a girlfriend, explaining that all the text messaging he's been receiving all night is from a stalker ex-girlfriend who just won't leave him alone.

The problem with this guy is not only his lack of honesty but a lack of character. Liars don't believe they have to take responsibility for their actions. Throughout his life, he's learned that he's gotten the best results by lying. So he uses lying as a tool to get what he wants. Being involved with a guy like this can do some serious harm to your ability to trust. Usually, when someone lies to you, you'll get a feeling like something isn't right. That's your intuition speaking. That's your gut trying to send you a signal that you should proceed with caution. The more you listen to it, the sharper you'll get at catching liars at their game. The problem starts when you ignore that signal; then it becomes quieter and quieter until it can't be heard anymore. The more you allow your own voice to become overshadowed by his, the more you'll get caught up in his web of deceit until it becomes painfully obvious that he's been lying all along. Then you'll feel like you can't trust anyone anymore because you can't even trust yourself. That's the kind of damage loving a liar can do to you. You lose faith in your own ability to sniff out liars. The good news is that, over time, you can begin to rebuild that trust again in both yourself and in time, other men.

The Cheater

The Cheater is like the Liar, just more pathetic. He cheats but isn't very good at it. He'll lie to you in order to facilitate his cheating, but he isn't very good at that, either. The women he cheats with are never as good as you are. You wonder why he does it in the first place, but he never has a good excuse. He can only sit there like a kid with his hand caught in the cookie jar. He scrambles to make excuses: "It just happened. It was only one time. You never pay me any attention anymore."

He cheats not because of you, but because of his ego. It makes him feel more desirable to sleep around. He also loves the challenge, because he has nothing to lose. When he hits on a girl, and she rejects him, it's, "So what?" because he still has you at home. But if he gets with her, then he's "still the man!"

Being cheated on hurts. There's nothing worse than that feeling of being betrayed. Afterwards, you're left having to make a difficult decision. Do you kick him to the curb or do you give him a second chance? That's a decision that a cheater forces you to make. If you have children involved, then it's twice as hard. Cheaters never really think about the consequences of their actions. They never really think about getting caught. Taking back a cheater can be a difficult thing to do. First, you'll have to get past the hurt and pain. Then, you'll have to trust the bastard again. Will he cheat again? Who knows? Some never do it again while others … well, we all know about them.

The Abuser

This guy is a loser with a capital *L*. He can negatively impact your life like no other. The abuser comes in three forms: the Mental Abuser, the Physical Abuser, and the Emotional Abuser.

The Mental Abuser will play mind games with you. He's not only sneaky as hell but also scary as hell. Think Hannibal Lector in the movie *Silence of the Lambs* when you deal with this guy. Okay, maybe he's not as sinister, but everything is a mental game with this guy. He views life as a chess match containing a series of moves. He's into mind games, and he'll try to control you in the most subtle of ways.

Identifying a guy like him may be difficult if you tend to attract manipulative people into your life. And this guy is good—damn good. He's had a lot of practice; therefore, the telltale signs are minimal. You could be cruising right along with this guy without ever realizing that you're being manipulated. He's able to unleash his plan because of the trust he gains from you. The best way to uncover a guy like this is to pay close attention to his actions. Because his weapon of choice is mental, it'll take time to uncover his true intentions, but, in time, his actions will make it hard for him to hide. He may tell you one thing while his actions indicate something else. It's during moments like these that you should remember the old saying, "Actions speak louder than words." Also, listen to your friends. Friends have a way of seeing things that we miss. If you ever have a friend come up to you and tell you that they get a weird vibe from your guy, listen up! They may be onto something.

The Physical Abuser can be your worst nightmare come true. He is charming at first, treating you better than you've ever been treated. You won't believe your luck that you've found a guy like him. But if luck is what brought you two together, it'll only be a matter of time before your luck runs out. He's a ticking time bomb, slowly ticking away until the time is right. He won't show you his abusive side right away because he knows that if he does so too early, you'll never see him again. So he lets things slide. He lets you think he's laid-back while inside he's suppressing his anger. He waits until you're emotionally attached to him; once he feels he has you, he expects you to play the game *his way*.

Anything can set off a guy like this. Anything he perceives as an indiscretion can result in a backhand blow across your face or a very violent shake. It could even be as seemingly simple as him pinning you against a wall. Sure, he'll apologize and become sweet again—until the next time. If you accept his actions, he has then succeeded in creating a cycle that will have you sucked in and feeling trapped. Sadly, anyone involved in such a relationship needs help. Always look out for the signs and characteristics of this type of guy (like violent outbursts or making verbal threats of physical harm) and never stick around after the first display of violence. And if you're involved in such a relationship, try and get help. Tell a close friend or relative and call your local domestic abuse hotline. You can dial information for the number or check the yellow pages.

The last type of abuser is the Emotional Abuser. This guy seems to love you at first; then he begins to put you down. He will make you feel like you can't do anything right. He can be just as damaging as the other two abusers because he damages your self-esteem. He knows exactly how to make you feel lower than dirt.

Detecting a guy like this can be difficult. One way he may mask his agenda is by using humor. If you're with a guy that makes snide remarks that are hurtful then covers it up by saying, "I was just kidding," beware. Let him know that you don't think these types of jokes are funny. If he continues, because he can't help himself, you'll know who you're dealing with. If you're around a group of people, and your guy feels like it's the perfect time to break into a stand-up routine making you the butt of his jokes, then it's time to say bye-bye. This is a clear indication that he is insensitive to your feelings and uses poor judgment. If you're still having difficulty determining whether a guy that you are seeing is emotionally abusive or not, follow the general rule of thumb: if someone makes you feel bad about yourself, you shouldn't be around them.

The Noncommitter

The good thing about this guy (if there is such a thing) is that he isn't quite as damaging to you as the losers I've mentioned so far. This guy's problem is that he can't commit to a relationship. He'll hang out with you. You'll share great moments together. You may even gush to your girlfriends how perfect this guy is. But there's one thing you'll never get from him: a ring. He'll allow you to only get *so close* before he begins to pull away. Everything is fine until you begin to call yourself his girlfriend. That's one type of noncommitter. He's the minor leaguer.

Then there's the other type of noncommitter. He'll date you until the next millennium comes around—just don't mention the *M* word. He'll make up any excuse why he can't marry you: "I just want to make more money first. I'd like to get rid of our debt first. I'm just waiting for them to find Jimmy Hoffa's body first." The truth is, he may never marry you. This guy is a major leaguer in the noncommittal game. If marriage makes him fearful, you can forget about him ever asking you to marry him.

Listen closely to a noncommitter and *pay attention*. Pay attention to what he says about his past relationships. Pay attention to his age. Is he forty-five and never even came close to making it to the altar? When watching a chick-flick together, does he try to make a leap for the door when you begin to cry during the wedding scene? Don't try to force a noncommitter to marry you and don't try to change his mind, either. Leave him and try to find someone who actually *wants* to marry you.

The Bad Boy

Why in the world would you ever want to date a bad boy at this stage in life? If you're reading this book, you've probably had your share of the "I-don't-give-a-damn-about-anyone-else" type of guys. You know, the ones who do what they want when they want. They live life on the edge with no thoughts of tomorrow. They love adventure and living a wild and crazy life is very adventurous. Bad boys tend to appeal to certain women because of their rebellious nature. If you've been raised by a very domineering father or in a very restrictive household, the idea of hooking up with a bad boy might seem like the perfectly natural thing to do. It may seem like sweet revenge against the way you were raised but dating bad boys doesn't come without some pratfalls. Just don't ask one of them about fixed interest rates or a 401(k) plan because he'll tell you that he hated Spanish in high school and that he sucked at math. This guy is good for having fun only. Don't fool yourself into thinking he'd be good boyfriend material unless *you're* a bad girl—then it's a match made in heaven.

The Narcissist

The Narcissist is actually very funny. No, really! If you just sit back and observe a narcissist, he's really rather funny. You'd swear that he's starring in his own movie and you're just a lowly extra. This guy may be so over-the-top that you'll be looking around for someone like Ashton Kutcher to jump out at you and tell you you're being *Punk'D*, as in the MTV show. But sadly, there are no hidden cameras and guys with boom mikes hidden behind plants. It's just you and him. Well, really just him. You just happen to be sitting there. He could go on and on about his favorite topic—himself. He may talk for twenty minutes before asking you a single question about yourself. When you're done with your thirty-second answer, he's already thinking, "Enough about you; let's talk about me!" You could bring a cardboard cutout of yourself and switch places, and he wouldn't even notice!

I once dated (very briefly, I might add) the winner of a state beauty pageant. I hadn't even noticed that she was a narcissist until I realized that no matter what we talked about, the conversation always found its way back to her. I once remained silent during one of our conversations and mentally counted how many times she used the word *I*. I got to twenty-three before I couldn't take it any longer. I realized that she was better off dating herself. Then she wouldn't have to worry about interrupting her conversation just to ask me a question. Stay away from narcissists. They have nothing to offer you but a bio about themselves.

The Hamster-Wheel Guy

The Hamster-Wheel Guy isn't going anywhere in life. He's pretty content with where he is, because it's comfortable. He has a middle-of-the-road job that doesn't require much from him, and hey, he's outta there at five o'clock on the dot! He is in his mid-to-late-thirties and has an apartment that's finally his own only because his roommate decided to move to Argentina two months ago to follow his dream. He likes to go out drinking with his buddies on weekends, and his life is devoid of any ambition. If you ask him what he'd like for the future, he'll think about it for a minute, then try to impress you by answering, "World peace!" Having no ambition is never a good sign for any man. The Hamster-Wheel Guy is happy just to be spinning his wheel round and round, because, just like the little vermin, he hasn't quite figured out that he isn't going anywhere.

The Failure-to-Launch Guy

If you've seen the movie *Failure to Launch*, with Sarah Jessica Parker and Matthew McConaughey, you know the guy I'm talking about. This guy is well over twenty-one and still lives at home with his parents. These guys may be few and far between, but they're still out there, and you need to know what to do if you ever encounter one—*run*! Unless he's saving up for a mansion in Malibu (and you should ask to see the checkbook just to verify), there should be no reason for a grown man to be living at home. The only real acceptable reason is if he's taking care of his ailing mother. If that's true, then that's very noble of him. But if it's for any other reason, watch out! How does he expect to be the man of the house if you two ever decide to move in together or God forbid—get married?

Sooner or later he'll be asking you, "Honey, do you think they'll mind if we skipped the mortgage payment this month? There's this awesome stereo system I saw on eBay that I'd like to bid on." The good news is that the Failure-to-Launch guy isn't as bad as the Hamster-Wheel guy or the Noncommitter. He might have the most to work with and just in need of a really good nudge to get him out the house.

The Macho Man

Remember when the Village People sang about being a macho man? (In case you're too young to remember, there were these six ... oh, never mind!) There was a period of time when it was cool to be macho. Guys had images of John Wayne on their minds. Being macho seemed synonymous with being a man. Things have changed now, and men are more sensitive and not afraid to show it. But there are still a few macho men around who believe that's the way to go. Their philosophy is simple: I am man, and you are woman. I do manly stuff, and you do the rest! Be cautious of the macho man unless you like the kind of lifestyle where you stay at home to cook and clean and take care of the kids while he controls all the money and your life. You can never leave if things begin to go sour because you have no money of your own. So no matter how horrible things become, escaping that type of relationship is like escaping from prison. You leave with just the clothing on your back because that's all that you own.

Ten Ways to Sniff Out a Loser

1. Trust your own instincts.

2. When he tells you something negative about himself, believe him.

3. Listen intently.

4. Find out why his past relationship ended.

5. Don't fall too fast. Take your time.

6. Ask questions until you're confident with the answer(s).

7. Observe his behavior.

8. Ask hypothetical questions to situations, then judge his response.

9. Do a background check.

10. Trust your own instincts!

Am I Attracted to Losers?

Take this short quiz to see where you stand.

1. You've just finished having dinner with a guy who asked you out when he tells you he'd like to go Dutch on the check. You:

   a. Tell him you don't mind because you *did* order that extra glass of wine.

   b. Pull out your calculator and divide the tip down to the last penny.

   c. Kindly pay your half and then make a mental note in case he asks you out again.

   d. Tell him you're going to freshen up first and then make a beeline for the exit.

2. You've been dating a guy for a month, and you notice he's quick to curse anyone whenever he feels they are disrespecting him. You:

   a. Try to see things from his point of view.

   b. Back away slowly so as not to seem like you are with him.

    c.   Tell him you don't condone that type of behavior.

    d.   Make matters worse by pointing your finger and yelling at whoever he's yelling at.

3.   You're talking on the phone with a guy you met at a bar recently when he starts to make sarcastic jabs about you and your appearance. You:

    a.   Tell him he has a wicked sense of humor.

    b.   Pretend you don't know what he's talking about.

    c.   Tell him you don't appreciate that brand of humor and that you'll hang up if he doesn't stop.

    d.   Laugh hard and then tell him a joke about his momma.

4.   The guy you've been dating for two weeks 'fesses up and tells you he has a girlfriend. You:

    a.   Tell him you won't tell if he doesn't.

    b.   Tell him he has to wear protection from now on.

    c.   Tell him it was nice knowing him and end the relationship on the spot.

    d.   Kiss him and tell him never to mention her ever again.

5.   You discover that the guy you've been seeing for three weeks hasn't worked for two months. You:

    a.   Wonder how he's been able to afford the double latté he drinks every morning.

    b.   Spot him money as long as he promises he'll pay it all back once he starts working again.

    c.   Tell him, "Sorry, but I like my men employed."

    d.   Keep seeing him, but only as a late-night booty call.

6.   Over dinner, the guy you've been hoping to get with for weeks tells you he believes that a woman's place is in the kitchen and her role is to serve her husband. You:

    a.   Tell him he's so cute that you wouldn't mind at all.

b.   Tell him you hope he has a strong stomach because you can't cook a lick.

c.   Tell him you strongly disagree and that he'd be better suited with someone more docile.

d.   Agree with what he says and then add, "As long as the woman gets to have a lover on the side."

How did you do? If you answered:

a.   *Score of three or more:* Losers must just *love* you.

b.   *Score of three or more:* There is hope for you yet.

c.   *Score of three or more:* You're definitely on the right track.

d.   *Score of three or more:* You may have to read this book twice!

Any other combination: You're love life certainly isn't boring.

Summarize This!

Life is a lot like that popular car commercial that goes, "In life, there are winners and there are losers." Not all guys are losers, but it can certainly seem that way if that's all you've been experiencing lately. The truth is, there are all types of guys out there. All of the good men are *not* all taken or gay. Like a good fisherman, you have to know how to attract the fish you want, and it isn't all in the bait. Half of it is in your head. It's important to change your mind-set in order to change your experiences.

This chapter emphasizes that you can't fix a problem if you don't know what the problem is. The problem isn't necessarily with guys but with your *choices* in guys. You can't control other people and what they do, but you can control your thoughts and actions and responses to other people. Whomever you end up with is *your choice.*

We are lucky to live in a country where we have the right to choose. There is power in choice. If you lived in a country where arranged marriages are still in practice, you wouldn't have much of a choice. The choice would be made for you. This is an absolute loss of power. Cherish this power you have and learn how to make choices that empower you instead of drain you. Wield this power carefully and do not take it lightly. The more you know yourself, the better decisions you'll make.

Famous Movie Bad Boys You Wouldn't Want to Date

1. *Hannibal Lecter.* Some women just *love* a challenge but not when their organs are at stake. Lose a challenge to this guy, and he'll not only take your mind, he'll eat your liver, too! [*Silence of the Lambs*]

2. *Norman Bates.* For all you women who love the silent types who love their mothers, beware! If his mother is also his only friend, there could be something very wrong with him. If you still can't resist, lock the door whenever taking a shower. [*Psycho*]

3. *Keyser Soze* It's always the sweet, innocent ones that are capable of the most sinister, compelling ... lies. Remember what Momma always told you, "Don't judge a book by its cover!" [*The Usual Suspects*]

4. *Nino Brown.* There's always an element of danger when dating someone who deals drugs. That element gets magnified ten times when that guy is trying to take over an entire neighborhood. A true bad boy to the fullest extent, you never know when Nino's going to do life in prison, but you know it's coming. [*New Jack City*]

5. *Max Cady.* It's admirable when people stand up for what they think is right. The problem is that some people take it a bit too far. Do this guy dirty once, and you might not live to tell about it. [*Cape Fear*]

CHAPTER TWO

IT'S WRITTEN
ON YOUR FOREHEAD!

There is a strange phenomenon that happens when two people are attracted to each other. Have you ever been strongly attracted to someone and unable to put your finger on why? Or have you ever been perplexed as to why certain types of guys seem to approach you as if you had a sign taped to your chest? There is a lot more that goes into attraction than anyone realizes. Sometimes it seems purely physical, and other times it's a deeper psychological force that is just as powerful as any other force in this universe. Attraction operates according to a Universal Law. Understanding how it works can give you an upper hand on how to use it properly and avoid being a victim to it. Here's a look at the different types of attraction.

The Physical

Let's face it—men are visual creatures. Their world is based on what they see. This is especially true when it comes to women. This just happens to be how most men are hardwired. Advertisers know this, and if you pay attention to ads, whether in magazines or on television, you'll be able to tell which advertisements were geared toward men and which were geared toward women. Marketing to men is simple and must be kept simple. Advertisers use lots of visuals that appeal to men, and the ad usually includes action of some sort. Comedy that consists of making someone look silly usually works well with men, also. And, of course, there are the ladies. Whether they're selling cologne or a car, there's always a beautiful woman not to far away.

Women, on the other hand, are different. Advertisers have to come up with ways that will engage as many of your senses as possible. A half-naked guy may make you smirk, but it won't make you want to sprint to the store. That's just one of the ways men and women differ. Men are visually influenced while women are more emotionally influenced.

So when a man notices an attractive female within his five-feet radius, he takes a quick inventory of his favorite ... body parts. "Boobs? Check. Hips? Check. Butt? Check! Okay, all systems are a go! Oh, wait. How about the face? Oooh, yeah! A definite go!" Now, it may not happen in that order. It all depends on what he sees first. If she's walking toward him, he'll check her face out first. If he's walking from behind, then you *know* what he's checking out.

This is the world according to men. These habits more than likely date back to prehistoric times when it was noted that man's best weapons were his eyes. He used them for hunting and to avoid being hunted. He also used them for choosing who had the best hips to bare his children. Not much has changed in two thousand years. Men still like to hunt (women) and still look out for predators (other guys serving as competition), and they still love hips on a woman (depending on the guy, this may have moved to the chest or the rear). So when it comes to men, physical attraction is very high on their lists, although this is only one form of attraction. This is probably the most dominant form for most men.

The Emotional

An emotional attraction obviously cannot occur between complete strangers. An emotional attraction usually occurs with someone you already know and have spent time with. This form of attraction is very powerful and can be very destructive. It releases neurotransmitters in the brain that can act like a drug. Once this attraction has been formed, the longer you are away from the person, the more you want to see them. These physiological reactions in the brain cause you to miss them so much. This works much in the way that bonding works. It is necessary in order for two people to want to continue to be together. That's why being in love makes us feel as if we are floating on air.

Problems with this form of attraction occur when one or both parties are already involved in committed relationships with other people or worse—already married. This is when an emotional attraction can be the most dangerous. This is how love triangles form, and you know how messy they can be. If you are the type of person who has trouble setting boundaries, you can find yourself in this type of situation quite easily. An emotional attraction can occur at any place and at any time, but it requires one key element: vulnerability. If the people involved happen to be single, then vulnerability plays a less significant role in the relationship. They aren't unconsciously seeking something they are lacking from someone else. It's knowing that you want something but also knowing that you should avoid it at all costs that adds to the appeal of this type of attraction. If you spend enough time with someone, you *will* begin to form some sort of a bond. Being single means there isn't already someone occupying that special emotional space.

But if you already share a strong emotional bond with someone, but that relationship is experiencing problems, you may be ripe for an inappropriate or potentially dangerous emotional attraction to someone else. This happens because your emotional needs aren't being met, and your existing relationship isn't giving you the same feelings you had before. Then you meet a new guy who gives you the emotional attention and support you used to get from your husband or boyfriend, and before you know it, you can't stop thinking about him or you wonder when you'll see him again. How far and how deep this attraction runs depends on your state of mind and the strength of your values. It is very easy to get sucked into an inappropriate or dangerous emotional attraction if your values aren't clear about monogamy and you have no set boundaries.

Many affairs begin this way. You see it often in the workplace where boundaries are relaxed and people spend a lot of time in a close environment. Workers sweat it out with each other. They form a camaraderie with their comrades in the next cubical. The high fives after a job well-done turn into hugs. The lunch breaks turn into meetings for drinks after work. Pretty soon a bond is formed and a pattern develops. Without a set of boundaries and values to serve as a safety net, you're capable of finding yourself starring in your very own soap opera.

Emotional attractions are very powerful and can sneak up on you very quickly. You must be aware of the possibility of one whenever you are going through difficult times within a relationship. Always set boundaries for yourself and make sure that your values are clear when you commit yourself to someone. Stick to your word, no matter how tempting.

There is another form of emotional attraction that occurs, and this one is usually one-sided. This form of relationship usually takes place in the mind of one of the individuals involved. There is a special name for these individuals: *stalkers*. A stalker can be someone you know or had a relationship with at one time before ending it or it can be a complete stranger. Either way, this kind of unwanted attention (and attraction) is never something to take lightly. If you ever find yourself in a similar situation and you are certain you are being stalked, it's important to let someone know (a close friend or relative). Then consider taking safety precautions such as letting the police know and varying your schedule times and daily routes.

The Psychic

No, I haven't lost my mind, and I'm not talking about dialing psychic hotlines. There is actually such a thing as a psychic attraction. It occurs between people everywhere, every day, all day long. It mainly consists of people reacting to other people's energies. Do you ever remember meeting someone for the first time, and for whatever reason, you just didn't like them? Or have you experienced the reverse: you meet someone for the first time, and after five minutes of talking together, you'd think this person was your long, lost twin? This happens because of the psychic connection you two are experiencing.

When people hear the word *psychic*, all these weird connotations come up. Some people have visions of a scarved lady, gazing over a crystal ball while telling you a bunch of stuff you already know about yourself. But one of the meanings behind the word *psychic* is "being sensitive to forces beyond the physical world." What that means in everyday terms is being sensitive to other people's *energies*. We all emit energy through our thoughts and emotions, and these energies are then contained in our auras. An aura is a body of energy that extends several feet beyond us, surrounding the entire body. We pick up on these energies every day without consciously realizing it. This is probably the single most reason people are attracted to one another, and it all occurs without anyone being consciously aware of it. Some very gifted people can read auras, or like me, can read people's energies (people who read auras can actually see the colors that make up an aura). This can tell you a whole lot about a person. You'll hear those who are a bit sensitive but not that experienced at reading people's energies commonly referring to what they are sensing as a "vibe." You may have heard your friends say they got a bad vibe from a guy that you are dating. If you pay close attention to how many times that has happened, you'll probably notice they were right most of the time.

The psychic attraction (or connection) can be seen clearly in the case of an abused person who attracts an abusive mate. The energies emitted between the abuser and the abused "match" each other, and unfortunately the abuser picks up on this energy subconsciously. That's how this attraction works. Another example of this kind of attraction occurs between couples who have been together for a long time or are really close. They can just look at each other and know what the other is thinking. Mothers sometimes experience this with their children. Remember when you would try your darndest to hide something that was bothering you from your mom and the moment she looked at you she asked, "What's wrong?" These are just a few examples of how a psychic attraction works. The key principle to remember when dating is that positive energy attracts positive energy and negative energy, well, attracts negative energy. So the next time you are sit-ting at a bar having a drink and waiting for a decent guy to come along, lean over and ask a friend, "How's my energy?"

The World's Best-Kept Secret

I am going to share with you the world's best-kept secret. I'm going to tell you how you can attract the man of your dreams, provided he's available and within reach. This secret is called the Law of Attraction. Sounds serious, eh? Well, it is, and—it works! I've used it, and some of my clients have used it. I'd love to tell you that I invented this, but it has actually been around for centuries. Even in the Bible it says, "Ask and it shall be given," (Luke 11:9). Like many Universal Laws present on this earth, we use it every day without thinking twice about it. Take a close look at your life right now and take an inventory of its overall state: happy, sad, miserable, pathetic, content. Now, take a look at everyone in it such as your friends or your boyfriend or ex-boyfriends. You've attracted all of this into your life in one way or another. From the condition of your life to your friends and boyfriends, they were all attracted to you by you. You've heard the saying that the mind is a powerful tool. Well, it's true, and your mind is also the architect of your life. Everyone and everything in your life has been drawn to you on a sub-conscious level. This goes for the car you bought last year and the friend you spoke with last night. They have all gone through your subconscious processing and have gained your seal of approval. Otherwise, you wouldn't be driving that car and that friend would just be another stranger passing in the night.

The flip side to all of this is that we also attract some of the crap we *don't* want. You're probably wondering to yourself, "This makes no sense at all. Why would we attract what we don't want?" Well, the mind is a powerful tool, but it may not always seem like a *rational* one. The conscious mind has a basic philosophy of avoiding pain and attracting pleasure, and you'll be surprised what some people will do to avoid pain and what others find pleasurable. When you're dealing with the subconscious mind, you are dealing with emotions—your emotions. They are like the fuel that runs this part of the brain. Think of your subconscious mind as a magnet that can draw to you whatever image you choose to conjure up. Behind that image is an emotion—either positive or negative—because this is, after all, how we experience life.

Now, if you think of something you don't want consistently, guess what you're going to get? Exactly! What you don't want. Your subconscious can't dis-cern that the image you hold in front of it is something you don't want because you keep it present in your mind as if it's something you desire. If you were to hold a magnet to a piece of metal, the magnet would draw that piece of metal toward it. Now, if you were to cover that piece of metal with some debris, the magnet will still draw the piece of metal, albeit with all the debris on it. It doesn't recognize the debris, but it recognizes the metal. It's just obeying the laws of magnetism.

Your subconscious mind works pretty much the same way. It will draw to you whatever you put in front of it (by way of your thoughts), and it will bring it to you. That's why they say, "Be careful what you wish for." This is exactly what they are talking about. Knowing how the mind works when it comes to relating to yourself and other people allows you to see things in a way you've never seen them before. Your dealings with guys won't seem purely coincidental anymore, and you will understand that you have as much to do with most of what happens to you as anyone else. This should give you the confidence to believe that you *can* change your life and get the results that you want. Now, let's take a look at how to make this law work for *you*.

There was this period when I wondered if I'd ever date a normal guy again.
All I ever kept meeting were these losers who wanted to go out with me.

—Amber

Attracting Mr. Right

Whenever I ask one of my clients what it is they want out of life, I am always amazed at how confused they become. They can run off to me an entire laundry list of things that they *don't* want. But when it comes down to what they really want, there is always a pause or some form of hesitation. They aren't even sure themselves what they truly want. You may have heard the saying, "If you keep doing what you've always done, you'll keep getting what you've always gotten." This goes for your thoughts, also. If you keep thinking about the things you don't want, you'll keep getting more of them. The key to all of this is to replace all of the negative thoughts you have about guys with positive ones. This goes for past experiences, also. You'll need to turn the negatives into positives in order to do this.

Within your memories of your past are stored emotions. If you're still pissed off and hurt over the boyfriend who left you for the waitress who worked at Denny's, you haven't resolved what happened to you. You haven't gotten past it, and you're carrying these emotions as a part of your energy. The guys that you meet may be similar to the guy that dumped you for Lindsey from Denny's because of your unresolved emotion. Remember what I said about attraction? Like attracts like.

What if you were to forgive your old boyfriend, and, instead of being left with anger, you were left with a peaceful feeling whenever you thought back to the relationship? What type of energy do you think you'd be giving off then and what types of guys do you think would be attracted to you? You see, it's all up to you and what you project. Everyone has experienced hurt and pain from a relationship. This is a part of being in love with someone else. But it is also possible to grow stronger and better from each and every heartbreak. If you can't, or haven't been able to, get to this point with any of your past relationships, you are sill holding onto the baggage from the experience. Your feelings are still unresolved. This energy is what's keeping you in neutral. This is what is attracting the same old things into your life.

Learn to forgive (although you don't have to forget) and let it go. Forgiving someone doesn't mean you are letting them off the hook. It's actually just the opposite. There is a big, bad force out there that turns night into day and causes volcanoes to erupt, so whatever you can imagine you'd like to happen to your ex, the force can do ten times worse. It's not about revenge. It's about karma. Get yourself to a quiet place and say out loud or within your heart and mind that you forgive so-and-so. If you still feel any hate and anger within you, say to yourself, "I really want to forgive so-and-so, but I'm still angry because of …" Getting in touch with the truth of what you are still feeling will allow you to begin to deal with it. Also, by saying that you would *like to* forgive your ex, you are putting your intentions out there, and the Universe will help you make this come to life. Carrying around old baggage from old relationships is slowing you down. It's keeping you from getting to where you want to go. It's dragging your energy down and attracting to you the wrong kind of guys. Do an emotional house-cleaning and get rid of all the junk. Throw out whatever no longer serves you and create room for new experiences, new opportunities, and new romances.

Now that you no longer wish that your ex would get eaten alive by a bear while camping, it's time to start thinking about what you want in a guy. What does your Mr. Right look like? (Be reasonable, there can only be one Brad Pitt, and he's spoken for at the moment.) What would some of his characteristics be? These are just some of the questions that must be clear in your mind if you want to attract the man you've always dreamed about.

In order to make things clearer, you must first make a list that will allow you to gain emotional clarity. You wouldn't go food shopping without first making a list. (Well, you could, but then you'd end up with a lot of crap you hadn't bargained for!) Now, this list *isn't* a checklist—by no means. You shouldn't choose a guy according to a checklist. It won't guarantee you'll make the right decision because there are too many intangibles that a list can't cover. The list that I'm talking about is to serve as your *guide*. It will steer your mind towards the kind of guy you want.

I've created a list of questions that will help you form a clear picture of the man of your dreams. Make sure you answer all of the questions on a piece of paper and keep it tucked away somewhere safe like under your pillow. Keep in mind when making your *own* list to include things in order of priority with the most important quality being on top. Also note how all of the phrases I use are written in the present tense. This is important because your subconscious mind works in the present. Using thought phrases such as "I am" or "I will" kick-starts the power of the command into action. In the Bible, there's an interesting verse that goes," If you believe, you will receive whatever you ask for in prayer," (Matthew 21:22). If you truly believe something, that thing will become real. Believe that Mr. Right already exists and it's just a matter of time before he materializes. Once you get to this point, you are halfway there!

The Mr. Right List
Answer these questions to create a picture of what your Mr. Right looks like.

1. How tall is he?

2. What kind of build does he have?

3. What kind of hair does he have?

4. List any facial features you prefer in a man. Example: he has a great smile with nice teeth. Or, he has the sexiest bedroom eyes. Be specific and don't hold back!

5. What does his voice sound like? Is it deep, or is it soothing?

6. What does he dress like? What's his style?

7. Is he a macho type, a metrosexual, or somewhere in between?

8. What does he smell like? Does he have the smell of your favorite cologne or plain ol' sweat.

Now, determine what characteristics he should have.

1. Is he kind?

2. Is he caring?

3. Does he treat you with respect? How so? Remember to be very specific.

4. Does he like animals?

5. Does he like kids? Does he want kids? Does he have kids?

6. Is he responsible?

7. Does he communicate his feelings well?

8. Is he smart? Is he artistic? Is he athletic?

9. Is he funny?

10. Is he sexual?

11. Is he motivated?

12. Is he romantic? If so, how romantic?

13. Is he predictable? Or is he spontaneous?

14. Is he independent? If so, how independent?

15. Is he honest? (Believe it or not, you have to write that down!)

16. Is he oriented to the larger family circle?

Remember to have fun with this list and go crazy. Can you recall when you were a child, and some adults in your life asked you to create a wish list? You probably wrote down whatever popped into your head. This is called writing without censoring. We censor ourselves too much and come up with reasons why we can't have something we desire. This exercise is a way for you to get away from censoring your thoughts and desires when it comes to choosing a mate. I know it can seem a little scary, but you have to think in terms of the big picture. What do you want in the long run? What do you believe you deserve? Write it down. Many people are afraid to write what they really, truly want because they don't feel they deserve it. Others don't believe it's possible for them. It happens to "other people" but not them. These fears are what's keeping them from attracting what they really want deep down inside.

Be as specific as possible when answering the questions. Don't just answer yes to "Is he caring?" Write down *how* he is caring. Maybe he cares about the environment. Or maybe he cares about people and mankind in general. Be specific in order to give your subconscious mind something to work with. If someone stopped you for directions to a specific street, you wouldn't just point straight ahead and say, "It's right over there somewhere." You'd probably say, "Head north about three blocks, then swing a left." Making this list specific also lets you feel like you're in charge. You'll limit the possibility of dating random guys who possess few of the qualities that are most important to you. You'll feel more in control of what happens out there in the dating world. This is all done by preparing yourself mentally so go ahead, and write it down. You deserve it!

Visualizing Mr. Right

Now that you have a clearer picture of what the heck it is you want, and your answer is no longer, "I want someone like my gay friend Johnny, but *straight!*" You are now ready for the next stage. This may seem a bit silly to you at first, but it works just as well as the list, if not better.

Visualization is one of the mind's most powerful tools, and I bet you already know this. How many times have you walked past a department store window and imagined yourself clutching that Chloe bag on display? Every time you walked by, you stopped and stared at it. Then payday came around, and out of the store you walked with your new bag in hand. You used your imagination to visualize yourself with the bag, and that started the wheels in motion. This is what advertising is all about. Department stores decorate their windows in the most fantasy-provoking ways. You may not walk in that day and purchase their product, but you'll walk away thinking about it. Then they let your subconscious do the rest. The more you think about it, the more you'll tell yourself that you've gotta have it.

Have you ever heard the saying," If you could see it, you could be it"? This is a direct reference to the power of visualization. Athletes use it to prepare for a game. Monks use it for world peace! Now you're going to use it to find Mr. Right.

The first thing you need to do is find yourself someplace quiet, somewhere you won't be interrupted. Now, according to everything you wrote on your list, conjure up an image of Mr. Right. Imagine yourself meeting him for the first time. Take mental notes of how he looks and how you feel around him. If there is an uncomfortable feeling that comes up, examine it. What is it trying to telling you? This is a good way to find out more about yourself and what may be some of the stumbling blocks that are getting in your way. Acknowledge whatever comes up and confront it.

Next, see yourself with Mr. Right, having a good time laughing and talking. This should cast a warm feeling around you and bring out some positive energy. Practice this often. This is a wonderful exercise that will expand your mind. You can do it before going to bed at night or before getting out of bed in the morning. Before you know it, you'll be attracting a whole new breed of guys!

> *All of my girlfriends have guys that they're happily dating, and I can't seem to find a single decent guy to go out with. Sometimes I wonder what's wrong with me?*
>
> —Tiffany

Summarize This!

Our great Universe is governed by its own sets of laws. Understanding how they work can allow you to work *with them* instead of against them. Being clear on what you want is the crucial first step. The next step is writing it down. The third step is believing, with 100 percent conviction, that it will happen. The fourth step is patience. With the rigidity of a mathematical equation, you must have all steps aligned in order to achieve your outcome.

Make your list and check it twice. Make sure it includes everything that is truly important to you in a mate and don't forget to list them in order of priority. If someone with brains is important to you, you won't want to put good looks first on your list with "smarts" being tenth, because you might end up with an Adonis who's happy just to get his first and last name right.

It's been said that we use less than 10 percent of our brains. Imagine what the other 90 percent must be like. Knowing this makes it easier to understand that our mind has the potential to attract whatever we can imagine having. This is all a part of our will, and we are creatures of free will. Free will is one of the most powerful aspects of being human, and many times we take it for granted. We may make decisions without really thinking things through. We decide things based on all of the wrong principles.

If you really want to change your life, whether in the area of guys or any other personal area, you must realize the power you possess. Realizing this allows you to take responsibility for your life. You won't view life like a crapshoot anymore where you are the victim to all that happens in your life. Seeing life through these fuzzy glasses leaves you powerless in the story of your own life. Taking the glasses off and realizing your true power puts the pen back in your hand. You will never be the only author of the story of your life because there is a higher power involved, but, heck, you could be the coauthor. You are the one making the decisions for your life. Learning how to make better decisions allows you to rewrite your life story and lead it to a happier ending.

CHAPTER THREE

BECOME A SHADOW CHASER

Dealing with the opposite sex can become very stressful at times. A lot of different thoughts can come up when you first meet a guy: *Does he like me? Do I look pretty? Do I look fat in these pants?* When you first meet someone you really like, it's as if you're sixteen again. Little insecurities can seem to seep out. These little critters can wreak havoc on your self-confidence, and if things don't go quite the way you'd like, they can make it seem as if you're spiraling downward towards a road to hell.

These little insecurities, which we'll call *shadows*, have much to do with why you choose certain losers to share your life with. The shadows' sole purpose is to follow you around wherever you go, slowly gnawing at your self-esteem when you need it the most. They can follow you for years, and if you aren't careful, you're entire life. There they will remain, inside your head, until you are ready to exterminate them. If you don't, they will take on a life of their own until they leave you with a carcass for a life. It's time to act like ghost busters and blast these shadows into oblivion! But before we can do that, we need to act like scientists and uncover where these shadows originated.

Mommy and Daddy Dearest

No two people have a bigger influence on your life than your mother and father. They can influence you either psychologically or biologically (through your genes). They can also influence your life through their presence or their absence. That's how powerful the synergy between parent and child is. When that X chromosome came into contact with that other X chromosome, you were born. With this merger came a lot of transferred data from both parties—some good, some not so good. In the same way you transfer files onto your computer, your genes became encoded with your parents' history. Then that magical day came. After spending nearly nine months in a protective sphere all by your lonesome (it's a miracle we aren't all claustrophobic), you were then delivered into this world.

Our parents, for the most part, had good intentions when they raised us. They raised us with no owner's manual, doing things the way *their* parents did them (or in some cases, doing just the opposite). Whatever they didn't know, they made up as they went along. This can only produce an imperfect childhood. Our parents may have inadvertently created our shadows by the way they raised us and the way they treated us. They served as our models of the world and also our programmers. As adults, our job is to undo any negative damage done in our childhood. We have to recognize the signs of where in our childhood things went wrong and where those effects still linger in our adult lives. Then we have to take the necessary steps to heal the scars of the past. Unfortunately, our childhood isn't the only area that can create shadows that linger inside of us. Any close, personal relationship can create shadows of its own.

The "Ex" Factor

Behold the power of the ex! An ex-boyfriend or ex-husband can magnify the shadows that live inside you, or he can create a whole new set of them. If life were like our school years, growing up with our parents would be like elementary school and the years spent with our exes would be like high school. If you think back to your high school days, you'll probably remember how much of a roller coaster it was. Being in a relationship with someone will expose the real side of you like DNA exposes a criminal. There won't be anywhere to hide, and when it's all said and done, you'll be left to sweep up the crumbs. If you've been through a string of truly bad relationships, you'll be surprised how much they can change you. You may not even be aware of the changes, because they happen over time. After a five-year relationship, you can end up a completely different person than when you began it.

This, in fact, is supposed to happen. You're supposed to grow over time. The ex factor becomes prominent if the relationship was an exceptionally bad or negative one. Then there's a good chance you came out of it *worse* than you were when you started it. Exes leave scars. They bring out the insecurities we carry inside of us. The shadows have a field day when a relationship comes to an end. But that's okay. The shadows are just that—shadows. In order to eliminate shadows, you have to know who you are inside. Just as important, you must know who you aren't. You are not your relationships. Relationships are experiences that *happen to you*. They aren't who you really are. You aren't a failure because a relationship didn't turn out the way you would have hoped. It ended because it was supposed to end. Once you're able to separate yourself from your past experiences, you won't be afraid to face your shadows anymore. Soon you'll want to thank your ex for all he put you through, although he'll be too clueless to know what the hell you're talking about.

The Friend Factor

Ever been burned by a friend? The pain can hurt more than a root canal without Novocain. When we bestow our trust in a friend, we have complete faith that they will never betray us in any way, but it happens. Friends can create shadows by proxy of just being our friend. They have access to our deepest thoughts and fears, and sometimes they can use this to their advantage. It all depends on the friends you choose. Friends are a wonderful and necessary thing to have in life, but you must take care in choosing them. Friends are, after all, just people, and people have their own issues and agendas. If you choose to be friends with someone who is known to be jealous of other women, there is a good chance she will one day become jealous of you. If you become chummy with someone who is known to stab people in the back, who is to say she will never do the same to you? I'd walk backwards, if I were you. Friends can create shadows that can last a lifetime and affect the outcome of future friendships. Treat them like relationships; choose carefully and learn from them.

Your Own Damn Factor

Guess who our biggest enemy can be at times? You guessed it—ourselves. As if we didn't have enough to watch out for! Like a dog chasing its own tail with the intent of biting the heck out of it, we feed our shadows until they begin to dwarf us. We are, indeed, our own worst enemy. We hear the voices of people long gone from our lives. We carry the torch of people who have done us wrong and parade it down the streets of our lives. It's been said that if you want to find the person who holds you back from being the best you can be, you need look no further than the mirror. This is the kind of power we have within us. We *create* our own heaven or hell. The thoughts that reverberate inside your head are no longer your mother's but your own. The ex who did you wrong is long gone, but his effect on you is enshrined, thus guaranteeing he will influence every relationship after him.

Our negative self-talk ensures that the shadows follow us wherever we go. They live as long as we continue to give them a voice. This is what gives losers a fighting chance. This is what gives them the opening to enter into your life. Change the negative self-talk (and thoughts) into something positive and empowering, and you'll shut the door on losers forever.

It isn't easy to stop doing something you've been doing for so long. You've probably been engaged in negative self-talk for so long, you can't even remember where some of the phrases originate from. This habit can take on a life of its own, and that's how they form the person you *think* you are today. But you are not the person you believe yourself to be if your shadows are ruling you. These shadows that whisper into your ear are just trying to keep alive old banter from people who didn't deal with their own shadows, and they passed them along to you. Like air into a balloon, their words filled your mind up with negative beliefs about yourself until your own shadow was created. Let's take a look at some of the most common shadows.

1) *I hate myself.* Self-hatred is very common. Sometimes this feeling can be so faint, you aren't even aware of it. But the signs are very obvious. Any self-destructive behavior can be a clear indicator you may be battling this shadow. This may result from a parent or guardian's abusive or neglectful ways towards you while growing up. Or it could be from feeling guilty over something that happened to you as a young child. Remember that children can't be responsible for events that take place. They don't have the mental capacity to be able to make informed decisions about things that happen to them, so stop blaming yourself. Adults who blame children for adult situations do so because they don't know how to handle the situation, and they want to deflect blame and responsibility.

How to face this shadow: Forgive yourself for whatever happened to you in your past. Understand that you couldn't be responsible because you were a child and that you are not to blame for what happened. This goes for anything you might have been through as a teenager or young adult as well. You must learn to forgive yourself and move on. *You* were the victim, but you don't have to live like a victim. Resolve to stop any self-sabotaging and self-destructive behavior and begin engaging in healthier habits.

2) *I'm worthless.* A lack of feeling worthy will have you walking around as if you were invisible to the world. If you become involved in a relationship, this shadow will make you a doormat. You'll wonder why people constantly step all

over you. It's because people will treat you the way you believe you ought to be treated. If you feel as if you have absolutely no rights, it'll be hard for someone to take a stand for you. This shadow can be a result of being put down continuously as a child. It can also stem from being physically or sexually abused, where your power has been taken away. The more powerless you felt as a child, the more worthlessness you'll experience as an adult.

How to face this shadow. You have to discover your own self-worth. No one can give you this. You have to believe in the core of your existence that you are as worthy as anyone and that you have as much right as anyone to do anything that you want to do, be think or feel. You have a voice, and it must be heard. You are *not* worth less than anyone, and no one is worth more than you, regardless of what you've been put through. *You are not your experiences.* They are just experiences that you've been through, but they are not *who you are.* Believing this has to start in the heart. You have to learn to accept yourself as a loving, capable human being. You must also practice speaking your mind and making sure you are heard. This may take some getting used to for both you and the people who know you, but in time it will become second nature. You can also write positive affirmations inside a notebook. Practice this daily until whatever you write feels perfectly normal.

3) *Why would anyone love me?* I call this the neglected-child syndrome. If you were neglected or perhaps abandoned as a child, then this shadow probably lives inside of you. The people who were supposed to love you failed you, and now as an adult you wonder how anyone can love you. Every child deserves and needs love, but because we live in a very imperfect world, terrible things like this happen. It may be hard to believe you can be loved for who you are if you've never experienced it before. Understand that you were failed as a child, but that doesn't mean you can't be loved. What your past means is that those who were supposed to love you were probably void of love. There are many adults who grew up feeling unloved, and they just pass that along to their children. Their own parents may not have known how to express love, and as the old saying goes, "You can't give what you don't have."

How to face this shadow. You must first learn to love if you want to receive love. You have to start by loving yourself. Think lovingly and positively about yourself. Learn how to cultivate the feeling of love within you. Practice loving your friends. Get a few plants or start a garden. Surround yourself with loving people. If it's possible, get yourself a pet. This can be an excellent tool in helping you to *feel* love. You can also sit quietly for a few moments every day and mentally send love out to the people you care about. Once you open your heart to send love, it will stay open to receiving love, and because love is a positive energy, whatever you send out, you will receive back. Also begin writing affirmations that describe you as a loving, caring person who is capable of giving and receiving love.

4) *I'm not pretty enough.* You've probably heard a million times before, "You shouldn't compare yourself to others," but you can't help it. You see other women out there, and you can't help but notice how "beautiful" they are. Then you think to yourself, "I can't measure up to them." This begins a vicious cycle that's hard to break, because it is, after all, a habit. But this habit is all based on illusions. Beauty itself is an illusion, because no one stays that way forever. Besides, it's also in the eye of the beholder. I know, yet another cliché—but it's true!

If you feel this way now, it could stem from not feeling like you were pretty enough as a child. You may have grown up being teased by the neighborhood kids or your older brother, and your parents did nothing. Your parent or loved one may have constantly compared you to a sibling or other individuals, which began a complex. If you were made to believe you were never good enough or pretty enough or were treated differently based upon your looks, then after a while, you may have begun to believe, "Maybe I am ugly." We could all have benefited from positive reinforcements as children.

The important thing is that now as adults, we define our own beauty. And this cannot and should not be measured up against anyone else. This must be defined by you. Aesthetic beauty is very shallow. Don't waste your time defining yourself against it. Everyone is beautiful in their own way. There is no universal code for beauty. It's all a matter of personal opinion, so focus on something that's more real—your heart. This is where true beauty lies.

How to face this shadow. Beauty begins from the inside out. Smile more and think positive thoughts. Stand in front of a mirror and learn to appreciate *all* aspects of yourself, even the less-than-perfect areas. It's you. It belongs to you, so spending time not liking something that's going to be around for a long time is a waste of time. Don't worry about other people's opinions. You can never please everyone, so you shouldn't try. Two people could look at the same thing and come up with two completely different opinions. The only opinion that counts is yours. Surround yourself with beautiful plants and flowers and notice how they are all beautiful and different. Practice being a more loving and compassionate human being, and you'll discover you have a radiant glow like no other. People will naturally be drawn to you because of your aura, and you'll just *feel* beautiful. Now let's see Revlon try and bottle that!

5) *I'm too fat and will always be fat.*—If you struggle with your weight, you know this self-talk very well. If you were a fat teenager, you know the script like the back of your hand. Your parents probably tried every motivational technique they could think of before giving up and trying to shame you into losing weight. "You're going to die if you don't lose the weight." "Who's going to want to marry you?" "Why can't you just stop eating so much?" Some people believe you can shame a person into losing weight, but that just exacerbates the problem. *They eat more* because they now feel horrible. They feel as if everyone has given up on them, so they give up, too. Before you know it, they're at three hundred pounds and considering gastric bypass surgery. This world isn't kind to overweight people, and growing up overweight can leave scars that can follow you well into adulthood.

How to face this shadow. You must first and foremost understand that you are not your body. Your body is merely your physical shell. Next, you'll have to confront the emotional issue that is causing you to overeat. What's been bothering you since you were a child? You may need to talk to someone about this. Therapy may be a good option here, because if you've been struggling with your weight for years, that's probably how long you've been struggling with the problem, too. It's never easy to go back to face a painful memory, but you cannot move forward until you go back. You need to break the cycle by confronting the problem. Food is like a drug, and many people use it to self-medicate. This form of medication is a lose-lose situation, because the problem will still be there when the food's all gone, and you may have a whole new set of problems—like poor health. Seek help if you need it and begin facing your shadow. Be aware that this shadow is from a long time ago, and things are different now. It'll be scary going back, but just like watching a scary movie, you can close your eyes and scream because it seems so real, but in the end it's just a picture on a screen.

◆   ◆   ◆

Fighting shadows isn't fun, but it's necessary work. You could look great on the outside, but if you don't quiet those shadows, they'll be whispering in your ear every time a loser comes along. And these shadows are *very* influential. Think of the devil-on-the-shoulder analogy: you may not want to date a loser, but because your self-esteem is so bad, it becomes a natural fit. His shadow meets up with your shadow, and they begin the dance of dysfunction. Take care of the things that haunt you, and believe me, losers will walk right on by, because their shadows will tell them they no longer have anything in common with yours.

Seven Things About Shadows That You Probably Forgot

1. Once you shine a light on them, they go away.

2. They're an illusion.

3. They can't hurt you.

4. They live in the dark.

5. They have no real power (only what you give them).

6. They probably aren't yours.

7. They may have scared you as a child, but you're all grown up now.

You've heard the saying "fake it until you make it." That works with some things but not when it comes to self-esteem. This is something you cannot fake. You may be able to get away with it for a short time. You might even be able to fool a few people along the way, but when the crap hits the fan, your ruse will crumble like a sand castle in water, and, believe me, it won't be pretty. Don't wait until you're in a relationship to handle the things you know might arise. Do the work *beforehand*. It's never an easy thing to admit our shortcomings to ourselves. And it can be frightening to face them, because so much emotion and memory can be tied to them. But if you don't take care of them now, they'll only pop up later, and I can assure you it won't be at the most opportune time. Take this time while you're single to do the work that needs to be done. Take as long as you need and promise yourself you won't start dating until you've started healing.

Summarize This!

Getting real with yourself is the only way to get better. Stop living in denial of things and stop sweeping old memories under the rug. These coping mechanisms only prolong the inevitable. You can't use a Band-Aid on a cut that requires stitches. It'll never heal properly, and the moment you bang the wound again, you'll open it right back up.

Heal the wounds of your heart by confronting them, then releasing them. Engage in some form of therapy by either speaking to someone, reading a book on the subject, or writing and drawing—anything that will allow you to get in touch with the inner feelings you are holding inside of you. If the problem is bigger than you, you may want to seek professional help.

Start today and don't let another day pass. Promise yourself you will make a change, and change will happen. Don't be afraid of the outcome but be present for the journey, because it is there that change occurs. It won't be easy. Sometimes you'll swear you were better off the old way, but the truth is that sometimes things have to get worse before they get better.

When you gut an old house, you get rid of just about everything inside. It may not look very appealing when everything has been striped away, but when the new material starts to go up, you can begin to see what it could look like. You must learn to develop long-term vision. When times get rough, try to see past where you are now and look at where you might end up. And always remember there's a light at the end of the tunnel. Sometimes you're just in too deep to be able to see it, but it's there.

CHAPTER FOUR

EXTREME MAKEOVER: THE NEW <u>YOU</u> EDITION

You did it! You've shed the old memories of losers past like the first ten pounds on a new diet. You've already been on fifty first dates with your imaginary beau, and now you're ready for the real thing to come along. But not so fast, sister! There's one more thing you should do before announcing to the world that there's a new sheriff in town. Get a makeover! There is absolutely nothing that will make you feel better about a new start than a head-to-toe makeover. I'm not talking about one of those makeovers when you walk out from behind a curtain and everybody's crying because they never knew you could look so good. I'm talking about a few subtle changes you can make that will let the world know there's a new girl coming their way and the old one is dead.

Getting made over not only makes you look great but also feel great. And since you've made all of those great changes on the inside, why not make some on the outside as well? Here are a few tips you can use to get started on your new makeover.

Is That Really Me?

The very first thing you need to do before you begin your makeover is to take an inventory. Don't worry; this won't consist of endless hours of counting dusty boxes. This kind of inventory consists of standing in front of a mirror. You may think you already know all there is to know about yourself like, "I hate my butt," or "My boobs are too small." But that's the wrong kind of inventory. With this, you'll be focusing on your *best* features, and here's a hint: we all have them. So before you start complaining that you can't find a single one, you need to look harder. Maybe it's your legs or your lips. Perhaps it could even be your neck. You are more than a butt and a set of boobs, and finding what works for you will make you feel sexier.

If you are still having trouble locating your best asset or assets, you can elicit the help of your friends. They'll be able to give you a list of things that are great about you. Sometimes we're so critical of ourselves, it makes it hard to see the good stuff. Little compliments from others tend to fall on deaf ears. Part of the reason for this makeover is to bring out a new, more positive you. After you've found what your best feature or features are, you are ready to let them shine.

A Girl's Favorite Words

It's time to go shopping! I bet those words are music to your ears. It's time to bust out the credit card and head to your favorite store. But before you go crazy and make like Bridezilla at a Vera Wang sample sale, remember you are on a specific mission. Your mission, if you choose to accept it, is to take the top-secret information you've learned about yourself and buy outfits that will accentuate your best feature(s). Just look for a few pieces that will go well with stuff you already have.

For instance, if your legs are your best feature, a nice pair of form-fitting pants will do. Jeans have been a hot item for quite some time, and just about everyone looks great in a pair of nice-fitting jeans. Look for the ones that have the best cut for your body type. Try on as many pairs as you need to until you find the one that's right for you, then buy yourself a few pairs in that style. It's better to have four or five pairs of jeans that fit you great than ten or twelve that don't. In speaking to many different women, they all tell me the same thing when it comes to jeans: They have a ton of jeans but end up wearing only their favorite pair most of the time. Save your money. Buy only what looks great on you.

Now that you have your jeans, you'll want to complete the lower half of your look by adding a new pair of high heels or stilettos. If a sexier look is what you want, the combination of jeans and heels are hard to beat. You can complete the look with a hot top, and you're almost on your way.

If a skirt is more your thing, make sure it isn't too short. It's always better to leave something to the imagination. Show off those legs without showing too much (i.e., a micro-mini). When you wear something that's too risqué, guys have more than getting to know you on their mind, if you know what I mean. They can't help it—they've seen *Basic Instinct* too many times. They're thinking, "Sex first, ask questions later," and that's not the message you want to send. You want to catch his attention *and* spark his curiosity at the same time. Keep it sexy but conservative. That's the safest way.

Oh, the Little Things

No outfit is complete without accessories. This could be a girl's best friend or her worst enemy. An accessory can either complete an outfit or ruin it. Well, it might not ruin it, but it could land you in the back of one of those magazines under the heading, "What Not to Wear." When it comes to accessorizing, remember one basic rule: *less is more*. I've seen too many women overdo it at times, and they wind up looking silly. When you have too much going on at once, you just end up looking like you have no taste. Yelling, "Hey, I was going for the bohemian look!" may buy you a moment of consideration, but we know better. Your expensive coif and freshly applied makeup will give you away every time. Stick to a simple necklace to highlight your neck. If you have a small or round face, stylish dangling earrings work very well. Try and stay away from the huge, obnoxious "chandelier-type" earrings that look like they belong somewhere in a dining room. I always expect women who wear them to say "darling" at the end of each sentence (I think I got that from my rich aunt while I was growing up). If you're into chain belts or waist belts, they also make a great accessory, but take care in choosing the right one. The difference can be between looking stylish and looking cheesy. Get the opinion of others on this one. Now, you're almost ready for a night on the town. There are just a few more things to do.

Beauty Tip: Want to Be Noticed More?

Keep accessories to a minimum. Don't let them overshadow you when wearing earrings, rings, bracelets, and necklaces. Accessories tend to draw the eye to a particular area. You want them to be a part of the show, not the main attraction.

Bring Out the Tresses

What else can make you *feel* like a brand-new person more than a brand-new haircut? A new haircut can do wonders for your look, not to mention for the way you feel. A great cut will have you strolling down the street as if you walked out of a Pantene commercial. The first step to finding a new 'do is finding a good salon. This may be easier said than done. If you already have a hairdresser who's been doing your hair the same way for years, it may be a bit of a challenge to get him or her to give you a completely different look. You may want to try a new salon and have someone new cut your hair. Either tell them what you have in mind and see what he or she can come up with or you can rip a page right out of a magazine and bring it with you. Just keep in mind that you need not make a drastic change in order to have a new look. For example, if you want change your hair color and feel like going drastic, try highlights first before asking for the whole bottle of peroxide. You don't want to go running from the salon in tears.

When sitting in the chair, tell the stylist you want a natural, easy-to-maintain hairstyle. The best ones are the wash-and-go types that just fall into place. Guys love natural-looking hair they can potentially run their fingers through. Nowadays, hair extensions are all the rage. Celebrities like Jessica Simpson and Christina Aguilera have used them to give their manes a fuller look. It has been a fashion secret for years. Hair extensions can be fun if you have a special event to go to and you want to spruce things up a bit.

Beauty Tip: Want to Look Taller?

Wear your hair in a high ponytail. This will help you create length as well as give your neck that elongated look.

Make Me Up

Now we're to the icing on the cake—makeup. And just like baking a good cupcake, you want to keep it light (unless it's Grandma's recipe). You don't want to *create* a new face, you simply want to enhance the one you already have. That means keeping it light and simple and natural like everything else. When it comes to makeup, less is definitely more. Nothing is a bigger turnoff to guys than a woman who wears too much makeup. They can't help but wonder what she looks like when she takes it all off at night. Wearing too much makeup will leave you looking like you're on your way to the circus to entertain a crowd of people.

For a fun and safe way to get a new look, head to your nearest makeup counter at your favorite department store. There, you'll find some of the biggest brands on the market. Many of them also have their own stores you can visit and receive a personal consultation. Just let the makeup artist or counterperson know what you have in mind (a natural look) and make sure they explain everything they are applying onto your face and why. Many of them tend to be heavy-handed, and if you aren't clear on what you want, they'll use your face as a canvas on which to experiment. Some of the best counters can be found at MAC (Makeup Art Cosmetics), Sephora's, Clinique, and Bobbi Brown.

Beauty Tip: Want Bigger Eyes?

Try using white eyeliner. This will give your eyes the illusion that they are slightly bigger and brighter than they actually are. Just be sure not to use too much. Then top it off with mascara as you normally would.

Going That Extra Mile

If all of this makeover stuff has gotten you inspired, and you want to do more, you might as well go all the way. You've taken care of your mental outlook and your appearance, now it's time to turn your attention to your body by beginning a workout regiment. If you're tired of being a couch potato, and every time you watch a Bally's commercial, you feel as if they're talking directly to you, then you're ready to work up some sweat.

Exercising adds value to your life by making you a healthier person. You won't look like you're on the verge of needing CPR after running half a block for the bus anymore. Exercise also releases endorphins that leave you feeling great afterward and is known to help with mild depression, too. You'll have more energy throughout the day and sleep better at night. And if that wasn't enough, you'll also look better in your clothes. Those stretch jeans will make you look more irresistible than ever! Do I need to say more?

Working out is the best gift you can give yourself. You'll feel more attractive, and feeling more attractive is the key to looking more attractive. You can either decide to work out at home or work out at a gym. If you prefer to work out at home, there are a thousand and one exercise videos for you to choose from, some with crazy-sounding titles like *Buns Of Steel*, *Three-Minute Abs* or *Ten Minutes to Better Thighs*. There are the perennial favorites that tone the entire body like *Tae-Bo* and *The Firm*. I have several clients who have experienced terrific results using these tapes. There are also low-impact DVDs like yoga and Windsor Pilates that may suit your needs. When choosing a workout video, find one that's fun and easy to do, so that you'll work out at least three times a week.

If you choose to work out at home, be prepared to be self-motivated, because you'll need a lot of discipline. I know too many people who buy a tape, and it ends up on the bookcase somewhere after a few workouts because all of their motivation is gone. Certain people really need a push, and that's why the gym may be a better option.

If joining a gym is the way you decide to go, signing up for personal training sessions is a very good idea (not to mention money well spent). If you've never worked out before and decide to go at it alone, you run the risk of injuring your-self by doing an exercise the wrong way. You may also wind up spending months seeing little to no results for all of your hard work. Many gyms offer free sessions with one of their trainers or an affordable package for a couple of sessions. This is a wise investment, and you don't have to "re-up" as they say in gym talk. (*Re-upping* means to renew your package.) What you can do is work with the trainer as they teach you the proper and most efficient way to work out. Once you feel like you've gotten the hang of it, you can go out on your own. Gym trainers know this. Their job is to teach you the right way of working out and the proper use of the gym equipment. If you get a trainer that's short on explanation and long on selling you a long-term workout package, ask for another trainer. The decision to buy more training sessions should be strictly up to you and shouldn't be discussed while you're working out. Some people like having a personal trainer because they know if they're paying for a trainer, they'll get their butts to the gym.

Beauty Tip: Want an Instantly Slimmer Body?

Try wearing a girdle or a body slimmer. Don't laugh! The ones available these days are not like the ones Grandma used to wear. This isn't a substitute for going to the gym, but if you need that extra boost of confidence for just one evening, go right ahead.

Dahling, You Look Mahvelous!

Want to look like a movie star? Do you want to look like you just stepped out of *US Weekly* magazine? There are a few simple tricks you can use to look like a movie star without spending thousands of dollars on a doctor in Beverly Hills.

One trick that will leave you looking like a movie star all year round is sunless tanning. This has been a beauty trick used by Hollywood's starlets for several years now. Just about everyone applies a sunless tanner; from J-Lo to Reese With-erspoon. It gives your skin that sun-kissed look without the harmful effects of UV rays. Just about every major cosmetic brand has hopped onto the sunless-tanning bandwagon, so you'll have plenty to choose from. I even saw one from a famous designer the other day. Take your time and read the label carefully before apply-ing. Be sure to exfoliate your skin first in order to slough off dead skin that can make your sunless tan look less than spectacular.

You can also opt for a professional spray-on tan, which I've heard works well because it comes out perfectly even. They even have do-it-yourself spray-on tans, but it can be difficult to apply yourself and can leave your bathroom a mess. You might have to experiment a bit before finding an application that works best for you. Skin bronzers are also very popular and are great when you need some instant color.

Beauty Tip: Tan Legs Appear Longer

Smooth, tanned legs appear longer and leaner, so it pays to give them a quick "faux tan" touch-up. You can use a spray-on or a self-tanning towelette. Try L'Oreal Sublime Bronze Self-Tanning Towelettes.

Another Hollywood secret you're probably already onto is teeth whitening. Just like sunless tanners, several companies offer teeth whiteners. There are toothpastes, paint-ons, trays, strips, and even whitening gum! I don't know if it'll make your teeth a shade whiter, but maybe it'll make your breath smell fresher! If you choose to whiten your teeth, you can either visit your dentist, who can lighten your teeth up to nine shades lighter, or you can choose an at-home kit. The at-home kit can get your teeth up to four shades brighter. Be careful not to overbleach (some people have been known to be addicted to bleaching) and follow the instructions carefully. For a super fast, easy-to-use kit, try Crest Whitestrips Renewal.

Your makeover is now complete. All you'll need now is to hire a bodyguard to keep all of those hot guys under control!

Six Ways to Tell You Really Need a Makeover

1. You've been cutting your own split ends since high school.

2. When watching old reruns of your favorite show, you point and say, "Hey, I have that same exact sweater!"

3. You've been doing your makeup the same way for so long, you could do it perfectly even during a blackout.

4. You get a ton of compliments when you wear something new to work.

5. You've worn your favorite top twice already this week.

6. You look at yourself in the mirror and think, God, I really need a makeover

More Beauty Tips

Check before you go. When wearing low-rise pants, check the mirror. Do a few bend-overs to make sure you aren't giving a free peep show. In fact, *always* check the mirror before going out. It's better to catch any mistakes at home than in the restroom of a public place.

Dance naked. Before a hot date, why not have fun and let your inner child out for a while? Before getting dressed, put on some great music and dance around nude. This will put you in a great mood and is sure to make you feel sexy for the night.

Shimmer, shimmer. If you want a little attention brought to your chest area (just a little attention), try adding a little shimmer lotion to add a touch of sparkle to that area. A little shimmer can go a long way, and it can make any area look more exciting. The trick is not to use too much.

You can't have it all. When deciding on choosing some skin to expose, choose one area—either your upper half or your lower half. This adds balance and assures you aren't showing too much skin. If you want to wear a hot, low-cut blouse, make sure to wear pants to cover up your legs. If you want to show off your gams, cover up on top.

David Blaine should try this. If you want the illusion of appearing thinner and longer, wear all one color. This is called the monochromatic look and should be done using only neutral, solid colors such as black, brown, navy, and gray. Want to look hot? Mix the textures up. Throw on a top that has a little leather on it. Break the boredom by adding a splash of color with a scarf or a thick, leather belt.

Workout Secrets

Chuck the scale. As a former personal trainer, I would always advise my clients to skip the scale, because the scale tells you so little about your true progress. In fact, it can discourage you in the worst way. There's nothing more discouraging than discovering you've worked your butt off for the past week and you managed to *gain* a pound. Trying to explain to my client that she actually lost weight but gained muscle was like speaking a different language that just didn't compute. All she knew was that the numbers were higher than they were yesterday, so she must be getting fatter. Avoid the scale. The true test of weight loss and progress should be how your clothes fit and how you feel. Losing inches is what weight loss is all about. Check on how loose your clothes are becoming. If they are getting tighter, then you are probably gaining weight, but if your pants are practically falling off of your hips, then you are on the right track.

Vary your workout. Don't just do cardio and don't just hit the weights. Vary your workouts. Do a few classes and make sure you vary them, too. Do kickboxing one day and take a dance class the next. If the weather is nice outside, throw on some roller blades and go blading. If you live near a scenic area, go for a hike. If a swimming pool is available, go for a nice swim. These all offer you a terrific overall workout, and they are fun to do. Working out doesn't need to be boring.

Stop smoking. Not only are cigarettes bad for your health, but they're also bad for your skin. You probably already know that smoking ages you, but did you know that carbon monoxide can contribute to cellulite?

Chill out. Stressing out makes you fat. No, really. Stress releases cortisol, which is known as the stress hormone. Cortisol makes weight loss harder because your body is primed for fight or flight. This type of reaction calls for your body to hold onto as much energy as possible (instead of burning it). After the threat is gone, the fat gets stored back in your cells. Learn how to better manage your stress in order to see better results in the gym. Go out with friends, journal, or, if you need to, see a therapist.

Get a massage. Getting a regular massage helps your body release toxins and lactic acid buildup, and did I mention that it feels "oh, so good?" Getting a massage is a good way to treat yourself after all of your hard work, and it also does the body good. It can help your body release stress in areas where you didn't know it hid.

Step it up. If you are always on the go, buy a pedometer. Experts say you should take at least ten thousand steps a day in order to achieve optimum health. A pedometer allows you to keep track of how many steps you accumulate throughout the day. There are simple tricks you can use to meet your "step quota." Take the stairs instead of the elevator. Walk instead of driving or taking public transportation. Walk briskly instead of strolling. Hit the mall on rainy days. All of these extra activities will add up to several extra steps per day.

Summarize This!

Your appearance communicates everything you feel about yourself. I'm not talking about being vain or being obsessed with appearances. I'm talking about the presentation of *you*—how you present yourself to the world. Which would be more appealing to you—someone who is dirty with their hair undone and holes in their clothing, or someone who is neat and clean and well kept? Manufacturers know they can have a good product, but if the packaging isn't appealing, their product will sit on the shelves collecting dust. It could be a wonderful product, but people will walk right on by because no effort was taken to catch their attention.

People can recognize hype, too. You can spend a small fortune on packaging and have a product that doesn't deliver. It'll only be matter of time before the word gets out. You *are* your own product. How are you going to represent yourself? What do you want your outward appearance to say about you? People respond to first glances.

Find out who you are first and then what kind of message you'd like to send. Does your look represent you? If it doesn't, change it. It's not so much about other people. That's secondary. It's about *you* first. How you feel inside generally reflects how you feel on the outside. It would be a shame if you felt great on the inside but your appearance didn't reflect that. It's time to get congruent about who you are and who you want to become. Sometimes a makeover can help you get to where you want to be (emotionally). So go out there and pamper yourself. Get your manicure/pedicure done and spend a full day at the spa. Schedule an appointment at the salon and make a plan to buy new makeup. Try new colors or a different way of applying your makeup. Join the gym and promise to actually *use* the membership. Take dance classes. Do whatever you need to do to break out of your rut. Then get out there and mingle. Meet new people who don't know this is your new look. Smile a lot and let the way you look match the way you feel, because, baby, you *are* marvelous.

CHAPTER FIVE

SEX IN THE CITY ...
OR COUNTRY

If you've ever watched a single episode of *Sex in the City* (starring Sarah Jessica Parker) in which she and her three girlfriends search for love in the big city, you know exactly how adventurous dating can be. Or perhaps your dating experiences could've been turned into a few episodes. In *Sex in the City*, all four of the girls are either single or involved in relationships that include their share of problems. In watching this show, it's clear just how different men and women are. Men are wired differently than women and share different priorities. Knowing *how* a man thinks and operates is what will allow you to have an easier time dealing with him. Just keep in mind that dealing with another individual, especially when matters of the heart are involved, is never without its share of challenges.

Different Aspects of Men

Men are externally driven. Men identify themselves by things outside of themselves. Who they are is defined by what they do, what car they drive, how much they earn, and what toys they've collected. This is also why some men require "eye candy" on their arm when going out. If you find a man who identifies who he is by the type of person he has become, you've got yourself a highly evolved male.

Men are highly competitive. Guys like to compete. Most guys grew up playing sports as young boys. Those that didn't were probably at home playing video games. With either pastime, there was a winner and a loser. Then in high school, a guy might have had to compete to get the girl he had his eye on. If he didn't compete directly with other guys, he competed to get her attention. Once adulthood set in, he's had to deal with getting himself a good job, finding a hot girl-friend, and winning against the musclehead who likes to park in his spot. When men walk around, they size up other men, whether they acknowledge this or not. They may not even be aware they are doing this because it happens so naturally. Watch what happens when a well-built guy walks into a restaurant. Most of the men in the restaurant will be aware of his presence. Men are always aware of potential threats to themselves and their women.

Men know what they want. Men generally know what they want. If you've ever gone shopping with a guy, he can get all of his shopping done at a department store in five minutes or less. He'll grab this and that (maybe he checks for the size or maybe he forgets), and then he's off to the register. He won't waste time taking a handful of items into the dressing room because he's got what he wants and they *look* like they'll fit. Guys see a car they like, point, and say, "That's gonna be my next car!" This is how most guys generally operate. So when a guy tells you he isn't ready or looking for a girlfriend, believe him. Don't try to change his mind and don't expect him to change his mind somewhere down the road. Take what he says at face value and operate from there.

Men are linear thinkers. Men think logically. They are not emotionally driven. This is not to say they aren't emotional. They just show their emotions differ-ently. Most of their decisions aren't based on how they feel, and that's a good thing or else they'd never go to work. Women are more emotional, and that fac-tors into the decisions you make. This disparity is necessary in order to add bal-ance in life. If everyone were emotionally driven, we'd all be walking wrecks. And if the entire world were filled with strictly logical thinkers, it'd be a rather dull and passionless place. Both aspects are necessary, and we all have the capacity to operate from both. It's the yin and yang of life. Which way you lean depends on your personal operating system. Men are conditioned not to cry while women are encouraged to talk about their feelings. This is why men have been so hard for women to figure out. They just don't respond the same way you would to certain situations.

Men have to be motivated. If you want to get your guy, or any guy, to do some-thing, you've got to find out what motivates him. Men do what motivates them and loathe what doesn't. If you want him to do something happily, find out what makes him tick. Most guys love football, so getting them to stay home on a Sun-day isn't that difficult. Tell a guy who just started working out again that he's looking great, and you've just encouraged him to get up at six in the morning for the next three months. Once you know what motivates a particular guy, you can get his attention whenever you want.

Knowing the basics of how men think should arm you with enough know-how to get out there and start dating with confidence. In sports, they say it's important to know your opponent. Once you know your opponent's tendencies, you can approach him differently. Dating is no different. Dating is a game. It's a let's-see-who's-right-for-me game. You have to do some work beforehand so you are prepared. Not being prepared is like taking a final exam without studying the night before. You do a lot of guesswork and hope you do well. Being prepared gives you the confidence you need to succeed with the opposite sex.

What You Need to Do *Before* You Start Dating

The first thing you need to do before you embark on the wonderful adventure we call dating is relax! Take it easy and have fun. People go on dates filled with anxiety and self-doubt, and that doesn't make the experience any more pleasant. It's just a date. You aren't committing your life away. If you don't like a guy, you don't have to see him again. And if a guy doesn't like you, he's freeing you up to be with someone who will adore you. This is the mind-set you need to have when you begin dating. Your mind-set has to be positive and supportive of yourself instead of in anticipation of a negative experience. Remember what you learned about the Law of Attraction? Your thoughts will create your experience; keeping them positive can only help you. Here are a few more tips that will prepare you for being your best when out on a date.

Come Prepared

Remember what I said about knowing your opponent and being prepared? If you've spoken to your date briefly over the phone or via e-mail, you should have a pretty good idea about who he is and what he does. You can take this information and formulate intelligent questions to ask when you're out on your date. Being prepared with interesting questions to ask *beforehand* will ensure that you aren't grabbing for questions during those awkward moments of silence. By being prepared this way, you can insure that the conversation will flow somewhat, and that you'll get to know your date even better. People love to talk about themselves, and asking him questions about what interests him will get him to open up to you. Before the night is over, he'll be asking you what you're doing tomorrow night!

Tips for Asking Great Questions

1. Ask questions and actually *wait* for the answer. Don't rush just to get onto the next question on your list.

2. Let the questions flow naturally. Don't become Barbara Walters or Diane Sawyer over the fried calamari. This will make him feel like he's being interrogated for a late-breaking story.

3. Know the questions you'd like to ask well and keep the list short (about five to seven questions). Then when you're out on your date, flow with the conversation. Stick to whatever the conversation is. You could be vibing so well you won't even need to ask any of your questions. Don't interrupt the conversation just because you haven't gotten to any of the questions on your list.

4. Keep the questions positive. This means asking questions that can only give you a positive response such as, "What's your favorite football team?" or "What did you like best about college?" Don't ask, "So, why'd you get divorced again?" Save this for the second date!

Never Let Them See You Sweat

Whether you're out with Mr. Hottie or Mr. Third Date This Week, always look your best. The expression "never let them see you sweat" means being cool, calm, and collected. You can't be the image of someone who's totally put together if you don't look the part.

Before you go out on a date, make sure you find out what the mood of the place you're going will be like. Find out what you'll be doing in order to dress appropriately. If he tells you that it's going to be a casual night at his favorite little restaurant, proceeded by some drinks at the neighborhood bar, dress a little bit better than casual. Wear your favorite sweater and skip the jeans with the holes in them. If your casual shoes have seen better days, stop by your nearest shoe-shine place and get a touch-up. The trick is to always look your best—even when the evening calls for a casual getup. But if he says casual, keep it casual but spiffy. You never want to look more underdressed than your date.

I remember going out on a first date once to dinner with a young lady. It wasn't a five-star type of night, but it was dinner, nonetheless. I'd worn a pair of slacks with dress boots to go along with a nice shirt. She came to dinner in a pair of sneakers she'd probably worn to the gym that morning, a pair of jeans, and a sweater that was two sizes too big. I couldn't get over the fact that we looked totally mismatched, and I wondered if she was aware that this was our *first* date? This was not a good way to make a first impression. Don't let this happen to you. Show your date you've put some thought and effort into what you were going to wear. He'll definitely notice it.

> *My friend once hooked me up for a blind date with this guy that she works with. I was so nervous for the date that I thought I'd vomit. Then I stopped myself and said, "It's only a date." I went out and had me a blast. It was one of my best dates ever.*
>
> —Stephanie

Show Some Teeth

Want to look five times more attractive instantly? Smile! Smiling does a lot on a date. Not only will flashing your pearly whites make you appear more attractive, it will also calm those butterflies that feel like they're about to bust out of your stomach. Smiling is also contagious, so if you smile at your date, he can't help but smile back at you. This will make everyone at the table more at ease. Add a couple of glasses of wine, and you've got yourself a fabulous time! So remember, use Crest Whitestrips before your hot date and dab a tiny bit of Vaseline on your teeth before meeting to help you smile more easily (an old modeling tip). Then think of your favorite comedy. This will put you in the mood for laughter.

Superflirt

Ah, the lost art of flirting. Flirting is truly an art form, and no one can do it better than a woman. The woman who knows how to turn on the charm can melt a man on the spot. Men are suckers for women who flirt, but it has to be done in the most natural way or else you'll end up looking like you're putting on a show. I remember watching old movies and going absolutely crazy about the manner in which the women flirted. The old actresses in those movies always seemed so cool and in control and knew exactly how to look at a man. They'd even flirt with the cigarettes in their gloved hands. Today, flirting seems like nothing more than a few glances in someone's direction.

If you'd like to attract any man you want (provided he's available), learn how to flirt. I know too many women who insist on playing it cool, and they miss out sometimes because the guy they were interested in wasn't aware of it. Remember, guys are literal and direct. You have to keep things simple and basic for them. If you see someone you like, send him clear signals that you are interested. Here are a few tips you can try when flirting.

Make eye contact. This is the most basic fundamental of flirting. Look at your target three times, and each time let your stare linger just a little longer. Smile when you do this so that you won't look like you're wondering whether or not you went to high school with him.

Work that hair. You probably know this already or have done this on several occasions. Sometimes women have a tendency of doing this unconsciously. But nothing works better than a well-timed flick of the hair. When he's looking over at you, simply establish eye contact in return and, with a closed-mouth smile on your face, flick your hair with your hand and slowly look away. You only need to do this once. This is the clear invite to come hither. After that, it's anyone's ball game.

Use the magic touch. If you've gotten past the point of flirting from across the room, and you're actually engaged in a real conversation with your paramour, make sure you touch his arm a few times during conversation. Just a gentle touch will do while you're making a point or while you're laughing at one of his jokes. This gentle touching sends subconscious signals that say, "I like you." This just reinforces any feelings you'd like him to know.

Talk that flirty talk. There's a certain manner of speaking that can get a person you are interested in to like you even more. This probably takes more skill than any of the other techniques. If done correctly, you can form an instant bond with the person you're talking to. By talking flirty, I don't mean sexual innuendos. Talking flirty is like pacing and leading someone in conversation by conveying interest.

Here's an example. Your guy mentions that he likes to ride motorcycles because it makes him feel free. You could say something like, "Wow, I've never ridden on a bike before, but I'd *love* to taste the freedom." A sentence like this forces him to read between the lines. What you're really saying is that, "I'd like to take a ride with you one day," thus ensuring that you'd like to see him again. By using the same description of bike riding that he used (freedom), you're automatically talking *his* language. The poor thing has just been mesmerized by you, and his only recourse is to say emphatically, "Sure! I'd love to take you riding."

So, remember when talking the flirty talk, you are only suggesting that you like the person and that you'd like to spend time with them but you're going about it in a roundabout way. Listen to what the person is saying about himself and his interests and use some of the same key words he uses to describe himself and his hobbies. If a guy says he *loves* playing dominoes, tell him how much you *love* playing Scrabble. If he tells you how *great* his college years were, tell him how *great* your college years were, too. This is a technique called *mirroring,* and it helps to create instant rapport with the person you're talking to. The idea is to find things the two of you genuinely have in common. Don't make things up so that it seems like the two of you must've been separated at birth. Mirroring takes a bit of practice, but it works like a charm.

◆   ◆   ◆

Now you're ready to go out there and knock them dead. Your charm will be irresistible to men. You'll be able to walk into a room full of men with total confidence. Other women will have to pull on their men in order to keep them from gravitating to you. Your Friday nights are no longer Blockbuster nights with your Shih Tzu, Daphne. You are once again a dating girl with more dates than you can handle. But before you take that leap into the dating world, there are a few more things to keep in mind.

Dating Do's and Don'ts

DO look your best.
DO show up on time. Call if you're going to be late; then apologize again once you arrive.
DO call your date by the right name. If you aren't sure what it is, ask him again. Don't spend the evening calling him Sam when a quick peek at his credit card shows "Dan."
DO listen intently and open up. Share details about yourself but not too much.
DO bring enough money to cover your meal and cab fare just in case you need it.

DO approach your date with a positive attitude. No one wants to have a date with a sourpuss. Remember that he's out to have a good time while getting to know you. Leave your problems at home.

DON'T drink too much. This can only ensure that you'll make an ass of yourself.
DON'T eat with your hands. Show some class. Skip the ribs no matter how badly you want them.
DON'T belch or lose control of any bodily functions. Don't talk with food in your mouth and don't laugh so hard that the water you were drinking comes out of your nose.
DON'T talk about religion or politics unless you're a religious fanatic or running for office.
DON'T talk about your ex. If he asks, just tell him it didn't work out and you hope he's found someone else. Don't use this as an opportunity to bash him.
DON'T talk about marriage. You barely know his name!
DON'T talk about the ticking of your body clock.
DON'T go home with him if you'd like to see him again.

Summarize This!

Now you're ready to go out there and have some fun. Remember that dating is necessary in order for you to find the right one. If dating ever becomes a tiring and daunting task, you may be going on too many dates and not enough of them with the right people. It's good to date, but don't say yes to just about anyone who asks. You should have a clear picture of what you want by now so that you can wean out those who don't fit what it is you're looking for. Keep in mind that you are in the driver's seat and you *can* say no if someone's not right for you.

Dating with the right attitude is crucial. Go out there not expecting anything but a good time, and nine times out of ten, that's what you'll have. If a guy is great but not right for you, you could potentially have a new friend or you may even have a girlfriend who might think he's the cat's meow. It's all about options, and that's why we date. You wouldn't walk onto a car lot, point, and say, "I want to buy this car!" They'd suggest that you test drive it first in case there may be something you don't like. Bringing a car back can be a terrible hassle for everyone. Have a fun, lighthearted approach when it comes to dating. It's an opportunity to get to know someone and see if this person has the potential to play a bigger role in your life. If you ever catch yourself beginning to hyperventilate at the thought of meeting someone for a hot date, relax and say to yourself, "It's only a date."

CHAPTER SIX

LOOKING FOR LOVE IN ALL THE WRONG PLACES

How easy is it to find a diamond in a dirt field? Or how hard is it to find water in a desert? Is it possible to find Manolo shoes for under a hundred dollars? If you know it's next to impossible to accomplish what I've just mentioned, why in the world would you expect to find the man of your dreams at a bar? Each weekend, masses of people head out to bars and clubs in search of a good time and the possibility of meeting that "special someone." There's no doubt this environment will allow you to meet many different people, but there are two things that can work *against* you: alcohol and anonymity.

When you meet a guy at a bar, you have no point of reference to go by. He could be anyone. Then toss in a few Long Island iced teas, and you'll need to have professional interrogation skills to find out who you're really talking to. If you're looking for a stable, lasting relationship, a bar or club may not be the best place to look. I'm not saying you *can't* meet a good guy at a bar, because it has been known to happen.

What I am saying is it shouldn't be your *only* place to meet a potential mate. It's tough enough out there, and you want to give yourself the best chances to succeed. When you're out drinking, you only have a few moments to assess whether someone is right for you or not, and after a few cosmopolitan's, everyone starts to look good.

There are better places and better ways to meet men. Because what you are interested in is a loving, lasting relationship, you'll need to start with the basics. A relationship is a bond between two people. The more common bonds that you share with someone, the stronger the relationship can become. So where do you go if you want to meet someone with whom you could possibly bond? Start with your interests. Make a list of fun things and activities you like to do, then begin stepping out and doing them. The idea is that whoever you meet at least shares the same interest as you. This makes it easier to get to know the person, and you may discover you have a lot more in common than just that one interest. Let's look at some of the places and ways you can meet someone who has the same interests as you.

Join a Class

Taking a class is an excellent way to meet a guy and have fun doing it. It is the ultimate win-win situation, because you may meet your future husband while acquiring a new skill. It could be any kind of class such as a cooking class where you'll learn how to sizzle in the kitchen or a salsa dancing class where you'll learn to shake your hips next to the cute guy with two left feet (or the instructor who acts like Don Juan).

If you're the corporate type, and you're looking for the same, you could check your local college for adult classes that offer a variety of classes on business and business management. If you happen to live in New York City or Los Angeles, you could check The Learning Annex for classes on just about any topic you might have an interest in.

If you're the athletic type, you may want to look into joining a coed league. There are coed leagues offering sports such as volleyball and softball. The options are endless and the Internet can serve as your guide. All you need to do is find an interest and then get out there and do it. Don't hesitate and don't talk yourself out of it. Many people avoid doing what they'd like to do because they can't find anyone to do it with, but you are going to *meet* people there if you just get past the idea of going there alone. If you just get yourself there, you're guaranteed to walk out of there with a new friend or two.

Go Clubbing

I know exactly what you're thinking: "My clubbing days are over!" That may be true, but I'm not talking about clubbing in the sense of "my-ears-are-ringing-because-the-music-is-so-loud." I'm talking about joining a club that caters to your specific interests. There are clubs for just about every interest imaginable. If you like physical activity and pushing your body to the limit, you could join a running club or a bike club. If you love books, you could join a book club. There are also hiking clubs and sailing clubs. Just pick an interest, and there's a club out there with members who like the same thing. This may or may not produce a boyfriend, but at least you'll meet like-minded people, and those people may know a guy who might be perfect for you. The idea is to get out and get social. Get into the habit of meeting people and networking. This can only help to increase your odds.

Spread the Word

It's important that people are aware that you are single and available. There's no need to shout it from a mountaintop or to wear a T-shirt with "Hot, Single, and Ready" emblazoned across the front. But your friends and family should know you are ready to date. Let your co-workers know of your status, too. The more people that know of your availability, the better the chances they may know someone you might like to meet. It's like having a whole network of people working for you. You're also putting your intentions out into the Universe and the Universe is *always* listening. It's about being proactive. You just never know how you're going to meet Mr. Right. A "hookup" from someone you know is always better than being approached on the street by someone you don't know.

Give of Yourself

Volunteering is a great way to meet people who share the same values as you. Volunteering can offer you a win-win situation because not only are you doing something wonderful to help someone in need, but you'll also feel great about yourself in the process. And if you happen to meet a caring stud while volunteering, that's just icing on the cake. It takes a special kind of person to want to volunteer their time and energy to a cause that's close to their heart, so you'll have a special bond with whomever you meet.

This should make it easier to get to know him on an intimate level without any pretentiousness (unless he's fulfilling his court-ordered community service). Lots of people have met their mates this way, and the relationships tend to last longer. There are even volunteer groups that cater to singles such as Single Volunteers of New York City. A quick search on the Internet should garner a list of volunteer groups in your area. Pick one that's close to your heart.

If you're into politics, political fundraisers or campaigns are a good way to meet people who share your views. People who are involved in these types of fundraisers are very passionate about what they do and what they believe in. You can join a Young Democrats or Young Republicans group. This will allow you to get involved in fund-raisers where you can network and meet lots of people.

Joining groups and clubs offers you the *possibility* of meeting someone, but there are no guarantees. It allows you the opportunity to interact with people and have fun doing it. If you feel as if you've been stuck in a rut, this is a good way to start getting back out there while allowing you to get your feet wet. If you already know what you want and are ready to cut to the chase, then you might be ready for a more direct approach. Here are a few more ways you can skip the subtleties, aim your bow, and shoot straight for the target.

Dating Services. Dating services make their members fill out an extensive questionnaire covering everything from their favorite color to how many kids they'd like to have. Then they take all the collected data and see if there's a match in their databank. Then there are other services that arrange events, seminars, and singles nights for their members. There are some services that focus on sports, religion, and even professional status. Make sure you know exactly what you're looking for before joining one of these. Because of the popularity of these services, there are some that may be less than reputable and you may end up not getting what you paid for. Ask questions before signing up.

Speed Dating. Speed dating allows you to "interview" a potential date in six minutes or less. They ring a bell and you get to barrage the guy sitting in front of you with as many important questions as you can muster. When the bell rings a second time, it's on to the next guy. You can potentially meet dozens of guys in a single evening. The good thing about it is you don't have to spend an entire evening with just one guy. You get to see what's available, and you write down the ones you'd like to know better on a worksheet (everyone wears name tags so you know who's who). At the end of the night, you turn in your sheet and hope that the ones you'd like to meet wrote your name down, too. If there's a match, the organization contacts both of you so you can make arrangements to see each other again. The difference this time is that *you* establish your own time limit.

Online Dating. Online dating has really caught on lately. After having to fight the perception that only the desperate go online to date, roughly sixty million people log on each month. There are hundreds of Web sites that cater to every type of person imaginable. There's even a site for booty calls! Whatever you're looking for is out there. Some sites are free and others charge a monthly fee with a discount if you sign on for three months. The good thing about online dating is that you get to list exactly what you are looking for, and you have a level of anonymity. You log on and check your online mail. If you click onto a hot guy's profile and discover he's not right for you, you can just press delete. If you're interested, you write back, and the dialogue begins.

The unfortunate thing about online dating is that people tend to misrepresent themselves. You have to learn to read between the lines. Also, guys tend to post pictures of themselves from ten years ago and thirty pounds lighter. I've heard this complaint several times from women, so make sure his profile includes several different pictures instead of a single picture. Just like anything else, there are no guarantees, but Internet dating is definitely worth a try. Approach it with a positive attitude with no expectations, make sure you're truthful in your profile, and include clear, up-to-date pictures of yourself. Then get yourself a cute username that fits your personality and click away!

Eight Tips for Dating Safely

1. **Never get in his car.** Unless your date is an old friend, never accept a ride from a first date. Remember, even though you've completed your first date successfully, he's still technically a stranger.

2. **Always carry cash and a cell phone.** Leave nothing to chance. You want to be prepared and capable of taking care of yourself in case anything should come up.

3. **Tell a friend of your plan.** Let your closest friend know what you'll be doing that evening and where. Write down your date's name and phone number (and username if you met online), and leave it somewhere she could find it. Better yet, e-mail it to her.

4. **Meet in a busy, public place.** When meeting someone you've never met before and don't know that well, meet in a well-lit, public place. This way, you'll be assured there will be plenty of people around.

5. **Always arrange for your own transportation.** Know exactly how you'll be getting home, whether it's by car, friend, train, or cab. Make this clear at the end of the date so that he won't have other thoughts.

6. **Never give out your home address.** The last thing you want is for some guy you thought you'd like to start showing up on your doorstep. Keep this information private (as well as your job location) until you get to know him a little better.

7. **Dress on the conservative side.** You don't want your date getting the wrong idea.

8. **Do a quick Google search.** Hey, you never know what might pop up.

I've provided you with these tips not to make you a paranoid dater but a smart one. In today's world you never know who you are meeting with. People hide behind the anonymity of usernames and daily masks. Everyone has a history and there's no way to know all of the details right off the bat, so you want to err on the side of caution. You can still go out and have a good time just as long as you know your boundaries. Once you're comfortable with who he is, you can ease up on the precautions a little bit. Let your instincts be your guide and always listen to the little voice inside you.

Love Is in the Air and Everyone's Invited

Just when you thought you were the only one looking for love, check out some of these unique Web sites you've probably never heard of (and might never need):

www.littlepeoplemeet.com: Where four-footers rule!
www.tall.org/clubs/ny/tcnyc: If you've ever dreamt of dating Yao Ming.
www.click2asia: If you've ever dreamed of dating Yao Ming's much shorter brother.
www.gnym.us.mensa: For those who love exceptionally smart men.
www.conservativematch.com: For those who leave nothing to chance.
www.ldssingles.com: Even Latter Day Saints need love.
www.datemypet.com: Better hope Killer likes him as much as you do!

Summarize This!

Dating can be a wonderful journey of self-discovery if you approach it with the right frame of mind. Try to avoid attaching any type of expectation to any of your dates, and you'll enjoy them more. Dating is a skill, and like any skill, the more you do it, the better you become at it. You want to be skilled enough at dating so that you'll be able to know in advance who's worth dating and who'll likely be a waste of time. Be selective in who you date, but don't be so selective that you don't give decent guys a chance. Judging someone on their outer appearance won't provide you with the full scope of the person's heart and soul.

Also, remember to participate on your dates. Don't be a spectator just going along for the ride. Suggest places to go and things to do. Offer to pay for part of your meal so that he won't think you owe him anything afterwards or think you're a freeloader there just for the free meal. His reaction to your offer could also give you some insight as to whether he's an old-fashioned guy with class (it's fine if he agrees to let you leave the tip). Adopt a positive attitude, and your dating experiences should begin to improve drastically. Keep in mind that what you bring to a date will either enhance the experience or detract from it. You may not always click with the person sitting across from you, but you could always learn something from the experience. Keep an open mind and go for it! You have nothing to lose (except for a few hours of prime-time programming) and everything to gain.

CHAPTER SEVEN

CHOCOLATE OR VANILLA?

Imagine that you walked into your favorite ice cream parlor in search of your favorite chocolate chip cookie dough ice cream, only to have the guy with the funny striped hat tell you there's only chocolate and vanilla available. What would you do? Would you stand there at the counter trying to decide between your two new choices? Or would you smile at Ice-Cream Boy and tell him, "Thanks, but, no thanks. I really wanted chocolate chip cookie dough today." This is an example of the kinds of choices we're faced with every day. Many choices are minor like, "Should I wear brown or black today?" or "Do I want Italian tonight or am I in the mood for Chinese?" Other choices are major and life-changing like agreeing to a thirty-year fixed-rate mortgage.

Our choices form our lives. As an adult, everything around you involves a choice on your part in one way or another. If you aren't happy with your life at the present moment, you have to take a close look at the choices you've made. There is power in choice, and thanks to the generosity of this wonderful Universe, we are the only living creatures capable of enjoying this power. We have free will, which means we have the freedom to do what we want. We can have whatever we desire.

The law behind this power is: behind every choice, there are consequences. Some of those consequences may not be what we desire. This is a result of cause and effect. If you've ever dieted, you know this law all too well (if I eat that muffin now, that'll be an extra thirty minutes on the treadmill). Some people are terrible decision makers. Some people can make great decisions for others but poor decisions for themselves. There are people who make great decisions in every area in their lives except relationships and picking a mate. Decision making isn't always so clear-cut when it comes to decisions of the heart, but it's important to pay attention to your past history and try to learn from it.

If you have a history of dating a certain type of man, and it always ends up badly, maybe it's time to try something new. They say that past history is indicative of future behavior unless a dramatic change or intervention is involved. If you're reading this book, you already know you tend to date losers, and it should be pretty clear as to why. Now I'm going to show you how you can make better choices, so you can break that habit of offering your phone number to the next loser who asks. Let's first take a closer look at this natural power we possess and how to wield it to our advantage.

The Dynamics of Choice

I'm not quite sure when the power of choice first came into existence. If you believe in the Bible, it could be when Eve had a choice between what God spoke to her and that firm, juicy apple. If you are a Darwinist, maybe the choice was between getting eaten alive by a Tyrannosaurus or a Pterodactyl. The more complicated the world became, the more complicated our choices became.

Now that we live in the technological age, we are inundated with choices. We can have anything we can think of in any size, style, or color. If we don't like what we find here, we can go abroad in search of our desires. The Internet has put everything at our fingertips, all only a click away. Our decision-making skill is challenged every day. If we buy a ton of clothes we don't like, we can always take them back. If we can't afford to buy something right off the bat, we can always charge it. If we marry someone who we discover snores, we can get a quickie divorce. The impact of our consequences is minimal in our day-to-day lives, so we lose our skill of making good decisions. Sometimes we spend too much time making a decision on one thing and too little on another. I know women who spend more time finding the right dress to wear to a function than they do finding the right guy. They'll spend all day trying on different dresses, rejecting each one that didn't "fit right." The same woman will go to a bar and get swept off her feet by some Kermit with a few smooth pick-up lines.

The Fundamentals of Choice

Choice is motivated by desire. If you have no desire for anything, you have nothing to motivate your choices. Once a desire is identified, you have what we call clarity. You know what you want. Some things are cut and dry: you want a slice of cheesecake, go where you can find some, and voilá! There you have it. Other choices make you feel like you're on the set of *The Price Is Right* (let's see, Bob, I think I'll take what's behind door number one!).

When you're single, sometimes it's hard to tell a genuine stud from a joker, but if you've been out there dating for a while or around guys, you might have a pretty good idea as to who's who. If you've done some of the exercises in the previous chapters, you should know exactly what you want. It should be pretty clear to you what qualities you want in your man. You should know what kind of character you're looking for in someone. Now you've got to sharpen your decision-making skills in order to make the right decision for you. You've got to align your heart with your head, which is not easy. But with practice, it can be done. Start with what you *won't* put up with. Here are a few things you should never put up with no matter how hot the guy is.

1. *Someone Who's Rude to You.* If a guy makes nasty, underhanded remarks to you, and then tells you, "Babe, I was only joking," it's time to laugh all the way to the door. This guy is trying to undermine you, and you don't need that.

2. *Someone Who Looks Over Your Shoulder While You're Talking.* This is quite common. He looks as if he'd rather be talking to someone else while his eyes scope the room. He swears he's listening to every word you're saying while he's eyeing the girl in the red dress at the next table. Suggest that he take his ADD pill the next time he's out on a date.

3. *Someone Who Shows No Manners Around You.* If you're out on a first date, it's a little too soon for someone to be getting so comfortable around you that he thinks it's okay to fart at the table, belch, or pick his nose. Anyone who acts like that is taking you for granted, and that's never a good sign right out of the gate. He might've forgotten to say, "Excuse me," so you say it for him as you get up to leave.

4. *Someone Who Doesn't Return Your Calls.* If he takes several days to call you back, and he does this on a regular basis, you might not have read the book, *He's Just Not That into You,* so I'll tell you what you missed: he's just not that into you.

5. *Someone Who Lies to You.* If you listen closely to what a guy says, and you have a good memory, you can catch a guy in a lie. The truth is most guys may tell a little white lie sometimes. Maybe he never dated Miss Kansas but

some girl who got cut during the tryout competition. Or maybe he never starred on his high school football team like he claimed, but he did make it onto the field with thirty seconds to go in the team's last game of the season. You have to know what to let slide and what to challenge. Not everyone lies, and not everyone tells the truth. Be clear on your values and make sure there are no little white lies when it comes to those areas.

Make your own list of things you absolutely, positively will not compromise on when it comes to dating someone. Include things you know will be detrimental to you if you were to go back on them. These things should include your morals, values, and principles. If you are a drug-free person, then drugs cannot be a part of your date's vocabulary. If you believe in working hard to achieve what you want in life, a guy who's involved in the latest scheme may not be what you're looking for. If you want a committed relationship, the guy who talks about not being ready to settle down might not be the right choice for you. You have to be as clear on what you *don't* want as you are on what you do want. You should know these things backwards and forwards. Then you will know you have clarity.

Famous Bad Choices of the Stars

1. **Liza Minnelli and David Gest**

2. **J-Lo and husband #1 and #2 (and P. Diddy?)**

3. **Elizabeth Taylor and husbands #1 through #8**

4. **Denise Richards and Charlie Sheen**

5. **Mike Tyson and Robin Givens**

6. **Michael Jackson and Lisa Marie Presley**

7. **Carmen Electra and Dennis Rodman**

8. **Britney Spears and her *first* husband of only a few hours and Kevin Federline.**

See, even the stars make bad choices! Rejoice. You're going to learn how to make good choices or, at least, better choices. Making better choices won't guarantee that the next guy you choose will become your husband, but it will ensure you are at least on the right track. Everyone has made mistakes in their past. This is virtually unavoidable because dating and relationships are a learning process. Some of us require a *very* long learning curve. The first step to learning to correct anything is to find out what you're doing wrong and why. Here are a few things that can contribute to bad decision making.

Hello, How Can I Please You?

Do you bend over backwards trying to make others happy? Do you sacrifice your own happiness for the sake of others? Does it kill you to say no to someone's request? If you answered yes to any of these, you could be a people pleaser. People pleasing is a bad habit that can be difficult to break. You may be so fearful of saying no to someone and of them being upset with you, you find it easier to say yes and do what they ask. People pleasers hate the thought of having someone mad at them. They'll go out of their way to do someone a favor all the while cursing under their breath. They expect that the person they are trying to please will appreciate their efforts. The problem is, they rarely do. People pleasers tend to attract "takers" and the more you give, the more they take.

If you're a "pleaser," this may have begun when you were very young. Your mother may have used her displeasure as a way of making you feel bad when you screwed up. She may have acted like her world just ended if you dirtied your new dress after she asked you to be careful. Her famous words to you were, "I'm so disappointed in you." Seeing the disappointment on her face only made things worse. Then she may have treated you differently for a few days for emphasis. As a child, this could be excruciating because we all want to impress our parents. We want them to think the world of us, and if it takes doing a few things we know will make them happy, we'll gladly do it.

Equally as important is *not* doing things we know will make others upset with us. An example of people pleasing with the opposite sex could be giving a guy that you have zero interest in your number or going out on a date with someone because he "looked so sorry," and you felt bad for him. When you go out on a date with someone you aren't into, you aren't doing them a favor. You're actually doing them a disfavor by leading them on. They don't know you don't like them if you agreed to go on a date with them. No matter how good your intentions, no one wants to be a charity case.

Be true to yourself and get in the habit of only doing things you have your heart set on doing. You are precious and your time is even more precious. Don't waste it. Let the nonprofits handle the charities. Being true to yourself (and others) will require you to be authentic. This requires you to say no sometimes, and people close to you may not be used to it at first. They are so used to taking advantage of your need to please, they'll think they're hearing things. You might have to repeat no a few times to prove you haven't suffered a temporary lapse of insanity. Say no as often as you need to until they get the point. Don't get talked into changing your mind.

In the Mood for Love

Do you remember when Alfalfa of *The Little Rascals* sang, "I'm in the mood for love, simply because you're near me"? Some people are just hopeless romantics. They sing along to sappy love songs and cry at romantic comedies. Their idea of a fun evening involves candles, jazz, and a nice bottle of Merlot. There is nothing wrong with being a romantic. The problem is when you fall in love with falling in love.

Hopeless romantics can't wait to fall in love with someone, anyone who shows a bit of interest. They love the chemical feeling that being in love produces. It's been documented that when we fall in love, our brains releases a neurotransmitter called dopamine. This gives you that "rush" that's so intoxicating. Some people tend to be addicted to this feeling. Life is suddenly rosier. The sun seems brighter and the birds chirp louder.

If you're someone who falls in love too quickly, you may be in love with the *idea* of being in love. The need to feel this way can cause you to fall for someone too quickly before getting to know them well. This can feel like an incredible force sweeping you in like a whirlpool. Check yourself. Do you view love through rose-colored glasses? Are you able to see a person for what they are or what you'd like them to be? Being able to identify this pattern in yourself is an important step in trying to combat this. If you "love" being in love, try to remind yourself that you want to fall in love with someone who feels the same way about you. You need to separate the person from the feeling. It's about the person first, and the feelings second.

Filling a Void

We tend to pick people who have qualities we lack in ourselves. Sometimes we also tend to choose people who remind us of our parents. If you have unresolved issues with a parent, there's a good possibility those feelings could play themselves out in your love life. This usually applies to the father-daughter relationship, and for guys, it's the mother-son dynamic. If you have old, unresolved issues with your father, this can create a void deep within. Then when you become intimately involved with another male, that same void opens up, longing to be healed. This is a trap many women fall into. Your father never gave you the love and attention you needed, so you find guys who will treat you the same way. Subconsciously you believe you can win his love—the same love you weren't able to win as a child. You want to prove yourself worthy of love, so you take on the challenge of getting this man to love you.

In essence, you are working out some of the issues you faced as a child. The problem is, your man is not your father, and the only one who can help you resolve the void you have inside is the one who created it. Become aware of any issues you may have with your father and try to resolve them *before* getting seriously involved with someone else. You can do this by working with a therapist or if you are fortunate enough, with your own father. Healing this void properly will eliminate the need to love someone like your father, and you'll no longer desire guys who remind you of your dad.

Owner of a Lonely Heart

It's Saturday night, and instead of getting dressed to go out, you're stuck on your couch watching back-to-back reruns of *Will and Grace*. Your cell phone hasn't rung for a week unless you count your best friend calling to tell you about how great her date was last night. Hearing this just made you feel worse. It's official—you're lonely and feeling like a loser. Your life is making you depressed. You look at couples in the street with spite (get a room!), and you roll your eyes at the trailer showing the latest Jennifer Aniston movie. You begin to wonder, "What's wrong with me? Why can't I get a date?" This thought form is the kiss of death.

Feeling lonely is normal. We all go through spurts of loneliness, especially after ending a relationship. The trouble starts when you begin to identify your life as being a lonely existence. This type of feeling may cause you to begin shunning your friends and turning down requests to go out. Slowly, you can go from hot chick to hermit. Your lack of intimacy can create a mild case of depression, and the more depressed you feel, the less you want to go out. Your therapy then comes in the form of Häagen Dazs chocolate brownie fudge and *Seinfeld* repeats.

Unfortunately, there is no scientific way to tell when someone will enter your life. You could try reaching out to Sylvia Browne and ask her when you'll fall in love again or you could just go about your life, trusting that when the time is right, the right guy will show up. You've heard it said that when you're *not* looking is when you'll find someone. I believe this. I also believe you find the right person when you're ready for the right person. Use the downtime you are experiencing to work on yourself—make some positive changes in your life that will prepare you for your next relationship.

Also, you can use the free time as an opportunity to enjoy being by yourself. If you don't find being in your own company fun and rewarding, how do you expect anyone else to? Learn to love yourself and do things by yourself first. Then when someone shows up ready to enter your life, they'll just be the icing on the cake, not the entire thing. Telling yourself you'll be happy when you have someone is giving away too much power. You should never put your happiness in someone else's hands.

Start going out more with your friends and make an effort to become more social. Join a club or go out to different social functions with the expectation of enjoying yourself and being social, *not* meeting someone. Being out and about turns your focus away from what is lacking in your life. You'll notice that life isn't that bad just because you aren't involved in a relationship. By surrounding yourself with family and friends that care about you, you'll still feel a sense of closeness and intimacy that can be lacking when you're single and alone.

We Have Ourselves a Winner Here!

If you're one of the lucky ones who's been busy dating a bunch of great guys, making a decision on who's right for you to date exclusively (and possibly call a boyfriend) can be a little difficult. You may like one guy because he has a great body and nicely manicured hands. Then there's that second guy who has a great job and likes to pay his bills on time. Then there *was* that other guy that looked like Denzel, but you're not even going to go there (but a girl can fantasize, there's nothing wrong with that).

With all of the different qualities to choose from, make sure you're choosing what's most important to you. You may not find the guy who has all of the qualities you'd like, but he must at least have the bare minimum. He must have a certain set of qualities that will get him through the door. Meeting the minimum will ensure he has a foundation to stand on that you can build upon later. This foundation should include qualities you absolutely *must* have in a guy as opposed to the earlier list of things you had to avoid. This allows you to shape your clarity even more, to be clear on exactly what you like and don't like in a man. You'll know, with conviction and clarity, what you are willing to put up with and when you're willing to send a guy packing.

When we're single and out meeting people, it's easy to be swept away by superficial things. You may meet a really handsome guy and forget everything that you've ever been through (at least temporarily), or you could find a guy who's so funny and charming that you're thinking about asking him to your cousin's wedding next month. By making a list and checking it twice, you can still be swept off your feet, but you won't find yourself somewhere in the clouds. The list will set your boundaries and act as your safety net. I've created a short list of qualities that no sane woman should ever do without in a mate.

1. *Respectfulness.* Your guy should be respectful to you and others around him. Keep a close eye on how he treats the waitress or the valet. Some guys will make an extra effort to be nice to you because they are trying to get you to like them, but they will slip when dealing with other people because in their minds they don't count. You don't want a guy who acts nice to you but curses out the waitress for bringing the wrong dish.

2. *Kindness.* There's nothing wrong with a kind man. Some women are so used to dealing with jerks, they think that being kind is a sign of weakness. You deserve to be treated with kindness, which has nothing to do with being soft. A man can be kind but also know when to put his foot down. A man that can do this is a well-adjusted man. Someone who's kind is also compassionate and thoughtful. Who wouldn't want to be treated this way?

3. *Attentiveness.* If you ever find a guy who's attentive, you've definitely got a winner. You want a guy who's going to pay attention to you but not go overboard with it. An overly attentive guy can get old quick, and it's a sure sign he lacks self-confidence. But if you're with a guy who's doing his own thing but still finds time to be attentive to you, that's a huge plus.

4. *Active Listener.* It's sad this has to be listed as a quality in someone you're trying to get to know and is trying to get to know you. There are people out there that are so focused on what they're going to say to impress you, they totally forget about finding out anything about *you*. There are others who genuinely could care less about what's going on in your life because they are so into themselves. You'll recognize these people by mentioning something intimate about yourself and waiting for a follow-up question that never arrives. They may either follow what you said with a similar story about themselves or about a friend of theirs, or they may change the topic completely with a comment like, "This gazpacho is terrific! You really ought to

try some." You want a guy who's going to listen to what you have to say and then ask questions because he wants to know more. This shows he's interested in hearing about your life as much as he's interested in sharing his.

5. *Effective Communicator.* Unless you've been born with well-defined psychic abilities, it's hard to read people's minds. It takes a lot of effort to make a relationship work, and communication is the backbone to any successful relationship. If you're out with a guy who has trouble communicating in the early stages, what makes you think he'll get better once he's in a relationship and the pressure's on? Men are notoriously poor communicators when it comes to discussing their feelings. Most men will open up with a little work and a lot of patience. Once they feel safe enough to open up, they will test the waters to see how it goes. If they feel they can trust you with their feelings, then they will tell you almost anything. If you're out with one who's already open and willing to discuss what he's feeling, he's worth some serious consideration.

There isn't a magic formula that will guarantee you'll make the right choices in men every time. It isn't as simple as going down a checklist and crossing items off as you go along. Knowing what's important in someone you're looking for will give you a big jump when it comes to choosing the right one. It will take a lot of effort because it'll require you to use your head over your heart. You may have to fight the urge to go for the types of guys you always have in the past. Time and experience allow you to become better at choosing the right person for you. The better your choices, the closer you'll be to choosing someone you could spend the rest of your life with. It's always better to have a handful of potential winners to choose from than a ton of losers.

How Well Do You Choose?

Are you a pretty good decision maker or do you tend to pick guys the way you pick your Pick Six lottery numbers? Take this quiz and find out.

1. You meet a guy at a bar and notice his wedding ring. You:

    a. Keep talking to him, pretending you didn't notice it.

    b. Grab his ring finger and tell him what a nice ring he has. Then ask him if it's platinum or white gold.

    c.   Tell him you don't date married men and then excuse yourself.

    d.   Whisper in his ear, "What your wife doesn't know won't hurt her."

2.   While out on a date, your guy openly flirts with the waitress. You:

    a.   Join in and start making passes at her also.

    b.   Ask him if he prefers blonds.

    c.   Remind him he's out on a date with you, and he's being rude.

    d.   Ask him if he's ever had a threesome.

3.   While talking on the phone to a guy you just met, he begins making racists jokes. You:

    a.   Begin telling him *your* best racist jokes.

    b.   Suggest that he do stand-up comedy.

    c.   Tell him his jokes aren't funny, they're insensitive.

    d.   Give him more material by telling him of an ex-boyfriend you dated.

4.   While out having brunch, your date lets out the biggest belch, and then continues talking. Moments later, he lets out an even bigger one. You:

    a.   Try to compete with him by letting one rip that's louder than his.

    b.   Begin to laugh and offer him some water.

    c.   Say, "*Excuse me!*" suggesting he might want to try saying it next time.

    d.   High-five him and tell him that was a good one.

5.   While grocery shopping, the guy working the produce aisle begins making sexual overtures toward you. You:

    a.   Tell him what you'd like to do to him.

    b.   Eat a banana seductively in front of him.

    c.   Tell him to cut it out immediately, or you'll ask to speak with the manager.

    d.   Ask him if he likes carrots.

6. Your well-intentioned friend hooks you up with a guy who is more looks than brains. You:

   a. Tell yourself, "Well, you can't have it all."

   b. Avoid talking about difficult subjects.

   c. Wait until the date's over, and then call your friend to tell her she's never hooking you up again.

   d. Tell him, "It must be hard for you being so beautiful."

How you handle certain pressure situations is a good indicator of how well you can handle tough choices. The clearer you are on what you want and the more you align your behavior with your desired outcome, the easier choosing the right guy will become.

How did you do? If you answered:

a. *Score of three or more:* You tend to go along with any situation. You're game for just about anything. The problem may be that your love life is like a chauffeur-driven car. You may own the car, but someone else is doing the driving. It's time for you to get back behind the wheel and do some steering.

b. *Score of three or more:* You like to avoid conflict. You'd be a fine candidate for work at the UN. You need to become comfortable with putting your foot down and asserting yourself once in a while. Failure to do so allows your date to think you're a walking doormat. That's not a message you want to send.

c. *Score of three or more:* You are the real deal! You are clear and concise on who you are, what you want, and what you won't stand for. You can separate the deals from the duds. Kudos!

d. *Score of three or more:* Nothing rocks you. You can make light of any situation, and few are better at sarcasm than you. The real question here is: "What type of guys are you *really* looking for?"

Any other combination: You're probably the most interesting person you know!

Summarize This!

You know the old saying about hindsight being 20/20? How many times have you thought to yourself, "If I only knew then what I know now"? There is no foolproof way of making the right choice at the right time 100 percent of the time. But if you let your past experiences serve as a guide, you should have a clue as to what works for you and what doesn't. In the area of relationships, we tend to allow our emotions to make the choices for us. The downfall can occur if you have some healing that needs to be done. If you look to others for healing instead of doing it on your own, you'll be susceptible to choosing the same type of guys over and over again.

If you happen to be in a really good place (emotionally) and are excited about going out there and meeting someone terrific, then clarity in what you want is the tool you'll use the most. Who you choose to share your life with can be a life-changing decision, so give it all of your consideration. Having mental clarity about what you're willing to put up with and what you won't tolerate gives you the foundation you need in order to make the best decision possible. It gives you a "safe place" you can operate from. Having this to back you up gives you the confidence and freedom to focus on who the person is first, before entertaining any possibilities of getting together.

Accept nothing but the best for yourself. Don't settle for anything less than you deserve. Stay truthful and make every attempt to live authentically. Never compromise your morals or values. It really is better to be alone than with some-one who makes you feel bad or uncomfortable. Life is way too short to spend it with someone who doesn't bring out the best in you. Get clear on what you want, and then go about your life until it shows up. Remember to have patience. Any-thing good is worth waiting for, and that includes a good man.

CHAPTER EIGHT

SO ... WHERE'S THIS GOING?

Hallelujah! You've found yourself a wonderful man. He pays attention to you. He fixes you breakfast in the morning. And heck, he even goes out shopping with you (and he doesn't enviously eye the skirt that you just purchased—whew). This guy seems alright. You've got yourself a real keeper.

Now it's been almost three months, and you're curious about one thing: where is the relationship going? Are you just friends or is there more? This is the moment where everything changes. When to raise this question with him requires timing and care. If you ask too soon, things can become awkward if he isn't ready for a commitment (or isn't sure if he wants to commit himself to *you*). Asking too soon can cause him to start pulling away because things are getting too serious, even if you contend that you were just asking out of curiosity.

When to ask and who should ask first all depends on the situation. Ideally, you would love for a guy to take you out to a romantic restaurant and under the flickers of candlelight say, "I'd like you to be my girlfriend." That would be nice, but that doesn't even happen in the movies. Another option is to cruise right along without saying a word. He may not bring it up because you haven't brought it up, so you both keep trucking right along until something happens. You may be at a party when someone asks, "So, is this your boyfriend?" Or you may run into his mother and cringe while she utters, "So, Larry, aren't you going to introduce me to your new girlfriend?"

Who should ask depends on who wants to know. If you're happy with things being just the way they are, then don't bring it up. But if you want to make sure you aren't just wasting your time, then *you* should do the asking. You want to make certain you ask when the time is right, and the only person who knows when that is- is *you*. Take your time getting to know everything about the person you're seeing before rushing into a committed relationship. This can take a few months or longer. It all depends on the flow of communication between the two of you. Because a relationship can be so defining, you want to err on the side of caution. Each relationship we experience can have long-lasing effects in our lives. Take your time, get comfortable, and observe your potential partner in different situations. If you rush too quickly into a relationship, you might discover things you wish you knew before. Besides, what's the rush? If a guy really likes you, he isn't going anywhere. You don't want to force a commitment from him. You want him to be dying to commit to you. And most men don't commit quickly. They like to take their time, and so should you. Exude a positive attitude and confidence, and he'll be knocking down your door. Here are a few more tips on how you can get him to go from maybe to a yes!

Get a Life

At this point in your life, you should have an active social life. You should be going out with your girlfriends periodically as well as doing stuff on your own. This ensures you aren't by the phone waiting for him to call. You don't want to be the girl who's available at the drop of the hat. He needs to know he can't call you Thursday night to make plans for Saturday. If you allow this to happen once or twice, he may start taking you and your time for granted. If he calls you at the last minute for a date, let him know you already made plans and really *do* make plans. Don't lie because that would be manipulative and deceptive, and you don't want to become that type of person. *Find* something to do. Deep clean your rug, clear out your basement, color coordinate your closet—anything! This will let him know he needs to call you a lot earlier than a day or two if he wants to see you. This isn't playing a game, it's sending the message that your life does not revolve around him.

Go Slow, Baby!

As I mentioned earlier, take your time getting to know someone. If you're having a good time getting to know a guy, why rush anything? Guys are usually at their best when the stakes are low. You can ask him almost anything you want to know at this stage, and you should definitely take advantage of this time. Men tend to clam up when they feel pressured, and nothing can create pressure like the possibility of beginning a new relationship. If he's meant for you, and you two are meant to be together, then it'll happen. So sit back, relax, and take notes. You may need them later.

Let's Wait a While

When should you sleep with someone for the first time? Trying to answer that is like answering the Million-Dollar Question. No one can give you a specific time frame. This is a decision that really depends on you. What you should be aware of is what's at stake. Sex changes things. This is without a doubt. It can bring you closer to someone or change the dynamics of a relationship completely. This is why it's better to wait if what you want is a relationship with someone. Different emotions come into play when sex is involved, and if what you share with a guy is still uncertain or shaky, you may end up regretting it. You want to be completely certain that both of you are on the same page. The longer you wait, the more certain you'll become. Even if things don't end up the way that you expected (because we never know what the outcome of things will be), at least you'll know you were absolutely certain you were doing the right thing.

Don't buy into the belief that you need to sleep with a guy in order to keep him. If you think this way, then your self-esteem isn't where it needs to be. And if the guy that you're seeing thinks this way, then he isn't the guy for you. Sex can be found anywhere at anytime. You want something deeper than that, and rushing into sex isn't going to get you there any quicker. So, to answer the age old question, "When should you sleep with someone?" Do so when you feel emotionally ready. Let your intuition be your guide.

Relationship Pitfalls

One of the most difficult things to do in life is to maintain a happy, healthy, and successful relationship. There is no universal model for everyone to copy. We grow up either emulating what we saw around us as children or trying to do the opposite of what we witnessed. Then when we start dating we realize it's a lot harder than we could ever have imagined. Trial and error now becomes our best teacher, and we keep trying until we get it right.

For starters, the purpose of relationships is to provide us with the opportunity of growth—personally and spiritually. Each relationship you've been through happened because it was supposed to happen and ended because it was supposed to end. Some relationships last only a season. As we continue to grow and evolve and learn, we are move closer to finding the person who may be there for a lifetime. So don't beat yourself up over your past relationships. They happened in order to help you evolve. It's one way the Universe gets your attention and gets you to make changes in your mind and life.

No one knows for certain when they'll meet the person with whom they'll share the rest of their life. I believe this will happen once most of someone's personal lessons have been learned and he or she has made the necessary changes in his or her life. It's important to keep an open mind and willingness to take responsibility for your role in your relationships. As with the science of evolution, we are meant to evolve with and after each relationship. Hold onto this mind-set, and you'll start viewing each relationship as a gift instead of a curse. It's easy to blame the other person for what went wrong, and it's also easy for us to take all of the blame. Any relationship is a two-way street. Focus on the *lesson* and not the *person*.

In the meantime, here are a few things you should avoid before entering into your next relationship.

Unrealistic Expectations: We each have a relationship model in our mind. Yours could be one borrowed from your parents, which includes the way that you witnessed them interact with each other. Some people create their own ideals of what a relationship should be like. Unfortunately, we rarely meet anyone who can fit our model exactly the way we would like, and their inability to conform to what we'd like causes tension. When someone does something we don't approve of, we get angry at that person. The more they do what we dislike (or sometimes don't do what we'd like), the angrier we become. Having these expectations is unfair to the person you're with because it doesn't allow him the freedom to be himself. Having certain basic expectations is fine, even necessary, going back to what you would and wouldn't put up with. The expectations we are talking about here have to do with your relationship model. Having a stringent relationship model is like having a script and wanting the guy you're with do each scene as you wrote it. This approach allows for no improvisation. If he isn't nailing the scenes the way you'd like, you conclude he isn't right for the part.

Having unrealistic expectations like these sets you up for failure. It doesn't allow you the freedom to choose someone for who they are, and it doesn't allow the other person to be who they are. Love is about acceptance—accepting people for who they are with all of their shortcomings and imperfections. Don't confuse this with assessing values and character. We are talking about being okay with someone *not being perfect* in our eyes. You will never meet someone who is perfect in the sense of doing everything right and nothing wrong. If they have particular shortcomings you absolutely can't live with, then that's important to acknowledge. That's your choice. But imposing expectations on just about everything they do or don't do places too much stress on everyone and is a recipe for disaster.

Expecting Your Man to Change. This is one of the biggest mistakes women make. You meet a guy, you see things that need changing, and you believe you have just the plan that can get him to change. Slowly, like an artist with a slab of clay, you go to work, only to become frustrated with your man's lack of progress. The truth is that people change only if *they* want to change. Most people have to be motivated to change, and nagging isn't one of those motivational techniques. It is true that you can motivate someone enough to change certain things if you know how to reach them mentally and emotionally, and they are open to changing. But you shouldn't enter into a relationship hoping to change someone, because you could be in for a rude surprise.

When you're with someone and deciding whether you should proceed any further, ask yourself, "Can I accept this man the way he is right now?" That would mean accepting the good with the bad. If the answer is yes, then if he does change things about himself during your relationship together, that becomes an added bonus. There won't be the stress of wanting and waiting for him to change, because you've already accepted him. If your answer is no, then you may have to consider whether the relationship is right for you.

Seeing things this way also allows you to be true to yourself. No one is perfect. We all have flaws and things that we need to work on, but no one likes to have someone breathing down his neck, trying to get him to change. Let him change on his own in his own time. This is the only kind of change that will truly be lasting.

Trouble Negotiating. All relationships are a negotiation. We all have trade-offs within a relationship, or no one would enter into one. Relationships involve give and take—I do for you, and you do for me. Of course, most of this goes unspoken. It all takes place within the synergistic energy that forms between two bonded individuals. But because we are talking about two different individuals of two different sexes, sometimes that unspoken communication needs more definition. Lines get crossed and calls get dropped. If your partner isn't giving you what you want, you have to ask for it.

For the most part, women are givers by nature. This was nature's way of ensuring that babies wouldn't be neglected. Women give to their children, husbands, elderly parents, and others. Sometimes you're so busy giving and doing, you don't even realize you're not receiving. Then when you come to this realization, you become angry at your mate for not recognizing this and giving you what you need. This may sound unfair, but sometimes you have to ask for what you need. You may be thinking, "Why should I have to ask? I'm busting my butt over here, and he can't see that?"

Men aren't as intuitive as women. Also, their needs are different. Instead of a hug after a hard day, they need a beer and the TV remote. They don't realize that a beer and a half hour of ESPN aren't going to do it for you, too. Instead of getting upset because he isn't in tune with what you need, talk to him about it. Don't talk to him about it while he's winding down himself. Talk to him when he's not stressed out, and tell him what *you* need. Communicate your needs like a skilled negotiator. The art of negotiating is getting a person to do what you want them to do by believing that it's in *their* best interest. Make it a win-win situation so he doesn't feel like you're asking him to do another "chore."

An example of this could be saying, "Honey, I really could use a back rub today. What if I sit down in front of you? That way you could rub my shoulders while we watch *SportsCenter* together." How can he say no to this? He gets to watch his show and please you at the same time! Then be sure to thank him when he's done. He'll have no qualms about doing it again the next time.

Fighting Below the Belt. In the sport of boxing, a punch delivered below the belt will get you penalized. Do it a few more times, and you'll get disqualified. Hitting your opponent below the belt is illegal. Because it's his most vulnerable spot, they've outlawed hitting in this area. Fighting with your mate has to follow the same rules: no hitting in vulnerable places. If you're engaged in an argument with your mate, you have to fight fairly. This means staying on the topic at hand. Don't bring up old issues that have nothing to do with what the two of you are arguing about. Don't tell him about the time that he screwed up when you were on vacation. Don't remind him of something he mentioned two months ago that didn't sit well with you. Perhaps you've heard of the old wives' tale that says women never forget indiscretions, no matter how small. Learning to fight fairly will require you to deal with issues right on the spot. Don't let them carryover and fester. This will just intensify your next fight. As a counselor and life coach, I have learned to read between the lines, and you'd be amazed at what *isn't* being said when people are communicating. Initially, people tend to hold back their true feelings.

Listen to what he has to say before making your point (and really listen, don't rush just to get your point across). Fighting involves two people who have two different points of view. It takes understanding, patience, communication, and trust to reach a resolution—even if that means agreeing to disagree, which happens sometimes.

Cheer up! Did you see yourself committing every pitfall on the list? So what? This is a perfect opportunity to learn from your past mistakes about what *not* to do. This is just as important as knowing what to do. It's never too late to change and you can get better with each relationship. Now, let's take a look at the little things that you can do that'll give any relationship strong legs to stand on.

Don't Sweat the Small Stuff

You've probably heard the rest of the saying, "And it's all small stuff." You may not always agree that it's all small stuff, but a majority of things we make into big deals really aren't big deals at all. They usually have to do with our own personal issues. Nothing can turn a relationship sour quicker than having someone nagging about every little thing the other person does. If your mate does something that didn't bother you in the beginning while you had the "love shades" on but drives you absolutely insane now, you have to take a step back and ask yourself, "Is this really about the way he eats, or is it something else?" If you cannot find any deeper meaning relating to the issue, then ask yourself, "Is this *really* important?"

In the grand scheme of things, you may find that, although annoying, the issue really isn't something to cause a big stink over. You can mention it casually if it really bothers you, but don't expect him to stop doing it right away. Whatever he's been doing, he's probably been doing a lot longer than you've known him, so it could take some time for him to stop. But remember, with the divorce rate hovering around 50 percent, it's time that we reconsider what the small stuff are.

Communication Is King

You hear it everywhere you go: the key to a successful relationship is communication. The problem with this is that everyone understands this, but not everyone understands *how* to communicate effectively. Effective communication is a lot more than opening your mouth and speaking. Many people believe that if they just learn to talk, then they are communicating, and everything should be smooth sailing. Then they become frustrated because things aren't getting better, in spite of their efforts. I wouldn't call that effective communication. Communication entails quite a few things. It requires you to be a good listener. Those who believe that they are good communicators are probably good at saying what they want to say but bad at hearing what the other person is trying to say.

Another requirement is learning to understand what *isn't* being said. Men aren't the most verbal of communicators. Research shows women use more than twice as many words as men on a daily basis. Men communicate better through their actions. Learn how to read what his actions are telling you, and you'll understand your man better.

Another skill that's required in effective communication is learning to read between the lines. This is different than interpreting actions. This requires understanding what someone is implying through their choice of words. People don't always tell you everything that's on their minds. Sometimes they don't know quite how to formulate their own thoughts. Oftentimes, they hope that you'll pick up on what they're trying to say. If you learn to listen carefully, you'll be effective at reading between the lines. It takes a bit of intuition and a real effort to try to understand someone who likes to talk in this manner.

People who have difficulty expressing emotions or being vulnerable like to drop hints and clues, sometimes with the hopes that you'll understand what it is they are trying to say. Mastering this technique can be helpful in trying to catch a liar, too. People who lie try hard not to give up too much information, but if you are skilled at reading between the lines, you can catch a crook every time—or, anyway, most of the time!

Keep the Passion Burning

Most relationships run into trouble once complacency sets in. The relationship becomes like a job—very routine. Relationships must be managed, and that means keeping it fresh and interesting while avoiding redundancy and boredom. Life can become routine at times with work and errands, and if you have kids, this becomes even more of a challenge. Keeping the passion burning requires effort, but the payoff is tremendous. Go back to doing the things you used to do when you first started dating. Leave little "I love you" notes in his briefcase. Make a date night and don't tell him where the two of you are going. Be creative and do these things for the sake of the relationship. There are a lot of options out there, and you don't want your mate contemplating them because he's bored with you and the relationship.

I've had women tell me that they wish their man would put forth the effort, but if they left this up to their men, the relationship would probably crash and burn. Most men just aren't good at managing relationships. They are the hunters and the providers. They'll take out the garbage and fix your car. Just don't ask them to know what the relationship needs and to fix it on their own. Besides, it doesn't matter who keeps the passion burning as long as it's there between the two of you. You may also be surprised that once you start making the effort, he may just follow your lead.

Do You!

This may be a difficult habit for you to break, but you must never lose yourself within a relationship. Women tend to do this, especially when they are involved in a long-term relationship. You get so wrapped up in your man, and the further the relationship progresses (fiancé, husband), the more your life begins to revolve around "him" and "us." There's no longer a "you." It's crucial never to lose who you are, because this is *the* most important relationship that you have. Staying in touch with yourself allows you to keep your self-esteem healthy and intact. The better you feel about yourself, the more you have to offer. Women become altruistic and almost martyr-like when they love a man. You can love yourself *and* your man. You don't have to put him before you and your own needs all of the time. A relationship is a joint venture between the two of you. He has his life; you have yours. Then the two of you share something together.

Even if and when you get married, continue to do the things that you enjoy doing—without him. Go out with your girlfriends, go to the spa, take a walk in the park, or nestle on the couch with a good book. Doing "you" re-energizes you and helps you to keep in touch with yourself. If, for whatever unfortunate reason, the relationship dissolves, you won't be completely lost, wondering who you are without him.

Summarize This!

Relationships are challenging. There are no guarantees in this game of love, but that can also be the beauty of it. Each person you share your time, space, body, and life with will teach you about yourself and life in general. You can either develop your relationship skills and get better with each relationship, or you can blame the other person for what went wrong and continue to make the same mistakes over and again. Relationships require a delicate balance between you and the other person. The quicker you learn how to trust yourself and your decision-making skills, the better you'll get at choosing the right mate for yourself. Then, once you learn how to exercise your skill at compassion, understanding, forgiveness, and acceptance, being with someone else gets easier.

Throw out the concept of finding the perfect person and focus on finding a person who makes you happy. He may not pass anyone else's checklist, but he treats you well and makes you feel great about yourself. He respects you as well as himself, and he has the same morals and values that you have. This is the type of person you should be building a relationship with. No one knows how long a relationship will last when first meeting someone, but it's not for us to know. It's about the journey. It's about loving, sharing, and growing. If the Universe feels that you have more to learn, it may send you a new lover to teach you what you couldn't learn from the previous lover. A love may enter your life for a reason (which is brief), a season (which is short-lived), or a lifetime. The closer you get to discovering *who* you are, the more prepared you are to share your life with someone forever.

CHAPTER NINE

UNLEASH YOUR INNER VIXEN

Within each and every woman lies a vixen waiting to be unleashed. It doesn't matter whether you're tall or short, thin or voluptuous. There is a goddess that not only wants to be let out but needs to be let out. She resides within the walls of your sexuality. Sexuality is one of the most powerful human forces on the face of this planet. It is not only an expression of love but also a provider of life and a feeling of freedom. Sexuality is a spiritual experience. In some ancient cultures, it was understood that when the bodies of two lovers united as one, they were as close to God as was humanly possible. As a woman, this life force flows through you. This is why you are able to have babies. It is also evident in your monthly cycle. By tapping into this naturally present power, you can become the powerful being that you were meant to be and unleash the vixen that lies dormant within you.

In many ancient civilizations, God was believed to be a woman, the Divine Mother. We still use terms like Mother Nature or Mother Earth signifying the overseeing of the earth and the giving of life to all creatures. Because God or the Universe is the creator of all things, a woman who can carry this process *must be* very close to God. Some men are very threatened by the power of female sexuality. This is evident in many different cultures throughout the world. Women are still viewed as second-class citizens in some parts of the world that maintain old traditions. It's amazing how times have changed! The ancient Greeks recognized and celebrated the feminine power by naming and honoring certain goddesses. Today, many women still have to fight to be treated and viewed as equals.

Men may be so afraid of the feminine power because they may recognize it as being *real* power, not the delusional power that they hide behind. Men have a thing with power and being in control, primarily because they are so ego driven. This is why they compete over money, cars, sports, and women. In their world, the more, the better. This isn't *real* power because material things come and go, and the connections made with many different women aren't true love connections. Once these things cease to exist, men sense a loss of power. They may also feel powerless in the face of real power, and feminine sexuality could be classified as one of these real powers. This power, which I'll call the Power of Seduction, has brought many powerful men to their knees, from Caesar to Napoleon to Bill Clinton. All of these men fell victim to one thing—female sexuality and its modus operandi, seduction.

Seduce Him

Seduction isn't manipulation. Those two things are very different. Seduction is getting a man to do what he already wants to do. The only difference is that you're getting him to do it *your* way. When you manipulate someone, you are trying to get them to do something they don't necessarily want to do. The truth is, you cannot seduce a man who doesn't want to be seduced. Those that become seduced are willing participants in the "game of love." Men love being seduced. They secretly enjoy falling victim to this feminine power, partly because they are hardwired to do so. Another reason is because women are natural seductresses. This is the power that you were born with. This may be Nature's way of ensuring you'll always be able to get what you need. Men have always been the hunters and the providers.

In past history, women have always used their sexuality to get what they needed: a roof over their heads or food for their children. The men went out and got stuff and shared it with the woman who gave him what he needed—sex, companionship and offsprings. These were the roles back then. Today, things are much different. Women no longer need a man to provide for them the way they did in the past. But interestingly enough, men's needs have not changed much. They still want what they've always needed, beginning with sex.

The Art of Seduction

Mastering the art of seduction starts with mastering your own sexuality. Seduction isn't necessarily just about seducing a guy. That's just part of it. Seduction is about getting in touch with the feminine power you have inside you. It calls for being comfortable with your own sexuality. Have you ever noticed a woman who walked as if she were totally comfortable within her own skin? A woman like this exudes confidence and sexual freedom that everyone, men and women alike, can feel. It's in her energy and the way that she moves. You don't have to be a size six in order to pull this off. In fact, it doesn't matter what size you are, as exemplified by the successful, plus-size actress/comedienne Mo'Nique). It's all about the way you *feel* about yourself and your sexuality. A great seductress feels good about herself and about expressing herself sexually. She is in touch with her body and doesn't have any hang-ups when it comes to sex.

The art of seduction calls for you to love yourself first and foremost. Nothing good happens until this happens. Then you must love your body. Love your body for what it does for you (like housing your spirit) and the joy that it brings you (through amazing orgasms). You must get in touch with your own sexuality by knowing your body sexually and knowing what pleases you. You must be able to seduce yourself before you can seduce anyone else. Once you've reached this stage, then you are ready to share your gift of seduction with the outside world. There are many tricks and tools that you can use to help you get the job done.

1. *Dress Like a Vamp.* Dressing like a vixen doesn't mean dressing slutty or trashy. It's just the opposite. Women who dress and act this way just aren't in touch with their feminine power yet. They're giving it away instead of using it. To dress like a vixen or a vamp means to highlight your very best assets in the most appealing, take-no-prisoners way. If your legs happen to be your best asset, you'll want to get yourself the hottest skirt (a slightly above the knee skirt preferably) with a nice, long slit on the side that is going to highlight those sexy gams. If you really want to turn things up a notch, you could pair the skirt with lace stockings. Now that's how vixens do it!

If your chest is your best asset, you can wear a low-cut sweater or top, but remember not to show too much. Show just enough. A vixen doesn't give anything away for free—it must be earned.

2. *Turn Up the Attitude.* This doesn't mean have "an attitude." Don't make the mistake of walking around like you're the hottest thing in town. This kind of attitude is fake and creates false confidence. The attitude that you should have is, "I feel good about myself." Learn to walk around like you like being you and you wouldn't trade being you for anything else in the world. This type of attitude in a female is intoxicating. Guys will want to know what it's like being with you because you seem to enjoy it so much!

3. *Add a Pinch of Confidence.* You have to believe and have confidence that men are powerless against your feminine charm. This may be difficult to build up to, but a seductress believes that she can have any man (provided that he's available and interested). You have to trust and believe in your seduction skills in order for them to have the full effect. You have to believe that, over time, you can have any man that you want. Seduction doesn't always happen right away. A seductress is patient. She knows she'll get her man. It's only a matter of time.

4. *Create a Den of Love.* Your home is where you'll spend most of your time alone. If you want to invite your inner vixen out to play, you have to create a comfortable environment for her. This includes setting up the right atmosphere using candles, fresh flowers, aromatherapy, and soft music. Create an atmosphere of love even if you don't have a lover yet. You have to practice being your own lover first before you can be a great lover to someone else. This means knowing your body intimately and becoming comfortable with it sexually.

Feng shui—an art form that originated in China thousands of years ago—is another good option for those who need a system to follow. The theory behind feng shui is that our *chi* (our energy or life force) can become stagnant and trapped, thus affecting our lives adversely. When your home is in balance, your life will be in balance. Feng shui states that different areas in your home represent different areas in your life. Some of the cures for the bedroom include rearranging your furniture (the bed should be diagonally opposite the door), then adding crystals, mirrors, lighting, color, potted plants, and even water fountains. Your nearest bookstore will have several helpful books on the topic.

Finding Your Inner Vixen

As I mentioned earlier, you have a vixen that resides within you. You can call her your goddess, vamp, siren, or temptress. Call her whatever terminology you feel most comfortable with. She is a part of you. She is your birthright. It's a part of your womanhood. Men and society have tried to silence her because of the power that she possesses, but they cannot destroy her. Tapping into this power source can not only empower you but also help to heal you. But first, you must analyze what beliefs and barriers you have that are keeping your sexuality under wraps.

There are many influences that were created to keep a woman's sexuality under control. They range from religious (Good girls don't behave that way!) to societal (If you exhibit any form of sexual freedom then you must be a slut) to personal (I can't be like that; it's too naughty). There is a power struggle to suppress female sexuality that still exists today. Being a vixen and getting in touch with your own sexuality has nothing to do with you sleeping with men. That is, of course, your option. It's about getting in touch and being comfortable with your own sexuality and sensuality.

For some reason, that makes some men uncomfortable. One reason could be that this is one area in which they have absolutely no control. You are in the driver's seat when it comes to sex. You are the one who chooses yes or no to sex. Understand that religious beliefs, societal labeling, parental upbringing and life experiences can all influence how you view your own sexuality. Because this is your birthright, you are the only one who should determine how it should be viewed. Don't be afraid of it. Being afraid of it is like being afraid of your own shadow. As long as you are a female, it will always be a part of you, so stop suppressing it and start embracing it.

How Well Do You Know Your Inner Vixen?

Take this short quiz and find out.

1. You see yourself as:

    a.   Sexually free and comfortable.

    b.   Fairly comfortable but keep a shot of tequila handy just in case.

    c.   As cold as the refrigerator in your basement.

    d.   Samantha from *Sex in the City* has nothing on you!

2. Your idea of sexy bedtime clothing is:

    a.   A teddy or lingerie.

    b.   Your favorite bra and panties.

    c.   Sweatpants and a large T-shirt.

    d.   Clothing? Who needs clothing?

3. Your way of getting a man's attention is by:

    a. Walking right up to him and saying something sexy.

    b. Walking up to him and introducing yourself.

    c. Saying a quick prayer asking God to forgive you for all your sins.

    d. Pretending that you're having a heart attack and hoping that he knows CPR.

4. To you, talking dirty is:

    a. Saying the raunchiest things that you can think of.

    b. Using a few terms that you haven't used since high school.

    c. Talking before brushing your teeth in the morning.

    d. Like feeling right at home with a bunch of sailors during Fleet Week.

5. Your idea of a hot night is:

    a. A nice dinner with dessert back at his place.

    b. Dinner and Samba dancing with who knows what next.

    c. Dinner at your place with 100 percent humidity and a broken AC.

    d. Whenever you go out!

How did you do? If you answered:

a. *Score of three or more:* You know who your inner vixen is because she comes out to play every so often.

b. *Score of three or more:* You're ready to take your sexuality to a whole new level.

c. *Score of three or more:* We have a lot of work to do.

d. *Score of three or more:* They should consider you for the sequel to *9½ Weeks*.

Unleashing your inner vixen is all about your attitude—your attitude toward yourself, your body, your sexuality, and sex in general. If you don't feel free and comfortable about any of these, then you have to work to change your point of view. Don't let others define who you are and don't let past experiences shape your opinion of yourself. You have to take back control of your life, and you do that by taking control of your thoughts. You are who you are, and that has to be fine with you. Love yourself. Even the parts that you aren't so hot on, love them too. They are a part of you. If you can change them, fine. But if you can't, heck, invite them to the party, too. You have to adopt a who-cares attitude. You can't worry about what other people think. It doesn't matter what they think. What matters is what you think. What they think is none of your business. Be yourself and love yourself. That's the greatest gift you can ever give to you. Now, here are a few ways to get in touch with that inner vixen who's been screaming to be let out.

Get Comfortable with Your Body

A vixen is at ease with her own body. She is comfortable with the skin she's in. If you aren't comfortable with your own body, there are a few things you can do to ease your discomfort. First, without any judgement, try standing nude in front of the mirror. Take a deep breath, and think of your body as just a body. Look at your neck, your shoulders, arms, breasts, stomach, legs, and butt. If you *really* look at them, you'll notice there isn't anything unusually wrong with them. You may not think your body is perfect and that's because no one has a perfect body. Cellulite and bodyfat already occurs *naturally* within the body. We begin to create illusions that aren't there when we compare ourselves to other people. You are who you are, and that is good enough for you. Even if you have certain area's you'd like to improve upon, you still have to embrace what you have. It isn't half as bad as you probably make it out to be.

A second way you can get comfortable with your body is to walk around the house naked. You could also dance naked. I recently heard that actress Alyssa Milano likes to do her gardening topless. There is nothing freer than being in the buff and doing activities in your birthday suit. It takes your mind off other things. Just be sure to put some clothes on when you go to get the mail!

Know Your Spots

It's hard to talk about being a vixen without talking about masturbation. Some people are uncomfortable with just the sound of the word, but you cannot be a true goddess if you don't know what pleases you. Masturbation is perfectly healthy and a good way to know your body. This can help you feel comfortable with yourself and more able to tell your lover exactly how you like it. Masturbation is a form of self-love that allows you to be in charge of your own pleasure. Here's a tip: men *love* to watch a woman who knows how to please herself. It's a turn on for them to see how you like it done. This can make you a better lover, and it can also spice things up in the bedroom. So, it's time to shed some of those old inhibitions and taboos and learn how to get it on with yourself.

One way to slowly introduce yourself to the art of self-love is to create a little ritual. Create some quiet alone time and light some candles. Play some relaxing and romantic music while you run some warm water for a bath. Throw in some rose buds, if you have some, and watch them float in the water. Afterwards, rub yourself down with your favorite lotion or body oil. Then you are ready to explore everything your body has to offer. Remember—the key to being a great lover to someone else is being a great lover to yourself!

Watch the Pros

If you've ever been to a strip club before, you've probably noticed how comfortable all the women are on stage. They have absolutely no inhibitions, and they are completely free to pursue any fantasy they desire. As a matter of fact, their job is to create fantasies, and they're quite good at it. Men pay money—and lots of it—to observe these fantasies. If these women can do this for perfect strangers, why can't you do it for a guy you've been dating for two months?

If you'd like to get a front-row seat on how to seduce a man, go to a strip club and watch how the girls work their magic. Make mental notes about how they move, what they do, how they work their eyes. Know that you can do this, too, if you just practice a little. Next, go home and mentally rehearse what you saw and made notes on. Then pretend your man (or a man) is in front of you and begin working your body the way you saw those girls work theirs on stage. This is a guaranteed way to send any man's pulse racing. All it takes is a little bit of practice and an ounce of courage.

If being in the strip-club environment makes you uncomfortable, you can always rent a movie depicting this, such as *Showgirls* with Elizabeth Berkley and *Striptease* starring Demi Moore. These films should offer you a few tips and ideas on how to move, but nothing can replace the energy and experience of watching it live.

Take Lessons

There are classes that cater to the art of the striptease. The popular gym chain, Crunch, offers a class that mixes stripping with exercising. Belly dancing classes are extremely popular and offer the same essence as stripping. It's all about getting in touch with your feminine sensuality and allowing your body to move according to its own curves. Men go absolutely wild for a woman who knows how to move her body in a way that accentuates every curve in her body. You don't have to be great at it, just comfortable doing it.

There are also workout videos that incorporate stripping with breaking into some sweat. Carmen Electra has a line of DVDs that show how to get it on in the privacy of your living room (or bedroom).

Toys Aren't Just for Kids

The sex-toy industry is one of the fastest growing industries today. There was a time when it was thought that only freaky and naughty people perused these places. Now, it's perfectly normal to walk into a sex shop wearing a pair of khakis. Once you are comfortable pleasing yourself without the use of toys, you're ready to graduate to the next level—battery-operated devices.

Again, this needs to be a slow and steady progression. Don't jump straight into toys, because you'll be missing out on a lot of sensory feedback that toys can't provide. Your own hand and fingers are still the best tools, but toys can introduce you to a whole new world. The most common toy for a woman is a vibrator. Not too long ago, there were only a few options when it came to buying a vibrator. There was only a plain-looking wand that doubled as a massager. Walk into any sex shop today, and it may take you an hour to choose the one that you want. Some look like devices and some look like the real thing. Some are so small they fit onto your finger and others are so large that, well … let's just say there is something for everyone.

Sex toys are fun because they allow you to explore your sexual potential even further, and they can liven up things in the bedroom. Just make sure you wait a while before introducing one to your boyfriend. Men can get a little intimidated when sharing their space with things not attached to themselves.

Rent a Porn Movie

This isn't really necessary to unleashing your inner vixen, but watching one won't hurt. If you've seen one before, fine. But if you've never seen one, perhaps you should see what all the hoopla is about. Most men love watching pornography because of the fantasy that it provides (along with the titillation that comes with it). Being a vixen means having all the areas of sexuality covered. You don't want to answer no to, "Have you ever watched a porno before." A vixen would answer, "Yes, and they're wild and raunchy!" This will lead him to believe that you aren't freaked out by them. It doesn't mean you'll want them as part of your foreplay (the choice is yours).

By watching a tape, you'll be able to say, "Been there, done that." And you won't be too shocked by what you see if you ever find one in your boyfriend's DVD player!

Meet Your Dominatrix

For those of you willing to go all the way, there is one final area to explore—awakening your inner dominatrix. Beware, this isn't for the shy, timid, or faint at heart (some men may not be able to handle it). Within every female lies a *femme fatale*—someone completely capable of sexual dominance. You can call this the darker side of sexual exploration. Female sexuality is *very* powerful, and the more you tap into this energy, the more powerful you will feel.

Dominatrices make a practice out of "dominating" men. There are some men out there who enjoy being submissive to a powerful female. This is their fantasy. They love being told what to do and how to do it while being totally submissive. Many times, these men are used to having power and being in control in other areas of their lives, and they would rather relinquish this control sexually. For others, it's just their fantasy being played out. Sadomasochism (S&M) is primarily about role-playing in a safe and controlled environment. There is an understanding between the one who is dominant and the one who is submissive. Everything is discussed beforehand, because it is, after all, about fantasy fulfillment. The dominatrices in this world are usually known as mistresses. They are in complete control. Their tool of choice is usually a leather whip, but the options of sexual prowess are nearly endless.

If you'd like to explore this underworld, there are many books available on the topic. Reading up on it beforehand may be a good idea to prepare you mentally. If you aren't too turned off by what you see and read, you may want to pay your local sex shop a visit and see what's available. There are sex clubs set up specifically for sadomasochism. They are typically known as "dungeons," but they don't advertise. You could be standing right in front of one and not even know it. They are very discreet. You could ask someone who works at a sex shop for more information regarding the locations of these clubs within your area.

Try a Little Tantra

Tantra is the five-thousand-year-old esoteric art form of connecting with a loved one. The word *Tantra* in Sanskrit means "extension," as in the extension of oneself. Hindu practitioners taught Tantra as a way of reaching God through the union of two souls. In Tantra, sex is considered sacred and the closest way to unite the spirit with God. You can't do Tantra with just anyone. It has to be performed with someone you care deeply about because it's all about opening your heart and aligning your spirit with your partner's. This wonderful practice is all about a deeper connection. You may find Tantra classes at your local holistic center. If you live in the New York City area, the Open Center and The Learning Annex generally offer classes on the topic. You can also find several books and DVDs explaining Tantra, but I believe it is best to attend live classes with a partner.

Kama Sutra is another art form of lovemaking that's a bit more popular than Tantra. Its origins can be traced back to India, and it involves engaging in seemingly endless amounts of sexual positions aimed at closer intimacy with your partner. Kama Sutra revolves around intimacy but in a more sensual way. There are plenty of books written about it, and there was even a movie filmed about it, displaying the eroticism that surrounds this mystical and ancient art form. If you are inquisitive, you can rent *Kama Sutra* from your nearest video store. This can only serve as an introduction—there is a lot more to it than what you'll see in the movie (because of the ratings system).

Enter Nirvana

Now that you are on the road to a much better love life, keep in mind the importance of sex in a relationship. Sex is an incredible bonding tool if both parties are present spiritually and emotionally as well as physically. You have to remember to keep sex high on your list of priorities, because not only is it important to him, it's also important to the relationship. I know many women who begin using sex as a tool to get what they want in a relationship or to "punish" their partners when they are angry at them for whatever reason. This is mistreating sex, and it can cause eternal conflict within the relationship. Never use sex as a tool for manipulation, regardless of how tempting it is. Sex is spiritual, and it represents the state of your spiritual connection to your partner. It's a bonding experience. Treat it sacredly, and it will reward you in many more ways than you can imagine.

Summarize This!

Your sexuality is one of your greatest tools. Sure, you're intelligent, witty, maybe you can drive the hell out of stick shift, and you may even know the difference between a touchdown and a field goal. But the one thing you have that a guy can never possess and every man wants is feminine sexuality. This is that feminine energy that lives and thrives inside you as naturally as the blood that flows through your veins. The trick is getting in touch with this power and removing all of the stigmas that have been attached to it in efforts to quench it. This feminine power is something for every female to behold and every male to be in awe of. Any fear of it is lost only on the weak and insecure men who gain their power by trying to control and dominate the women they are with. If they would learn to embrace this energy and appreciate what it does to them, the synergistic energy that occurs between men and women would live in perfect harmony. Nature knows what it's doing. It wouldn't give you this power for nothing!

Get back in touch with this energy and feel what it does to you. Observe what it feels like and slowly allow it to reform and reshape your femininity. Allow yourself to feel sexy again. You don't have to walk around oozing sex. That wouldn't be too wise, but use it as a tool—taking it out whenever you need it. Remember, it isn't about manipulation. Never try to get someone to do something they are against or morally opposed to. Sharing your feminine energy is more like giving a guy a small gift. You're giving him a peek at your most feminine ways. It's a lot like throwing a dog a small bone—it isn't quite feeding time, but a small bone will keep him satisfied for awhile!

CONCLUSION

WATCH OUT, WORLD!

Congratulations! You have completed your education of *How to Stop Dating Losers Forever!* You did the work, and you chased away a few shadows. You were able to meet your inner vixen, and you feel comfortable and free within your own flesh. Your walk has more bounce, and your step has more pep. You exude a new aura of confidence. You also realize that happiness resides within you. You understand that happiness is *your* responsibility, and not anyone else's.

I've provided you, within this book, enough tools to turn things around in your life. Remember that life always comes down to one thing—choices. Knowing this can save us from a lot of unnecessary heartache and repetitive torture. You won't ever make perfect choices, but you can aim to make the best choices available to you. No matter who you end up with, there will always be challenges to face and hurdles to leap, but with each challenge and hurdle you conquer, there is a reward—growth. Don't be afraid of growing. It is the natural progression of all living things. The growth I'm referring to in this case is spiritual growth. Relationships are all about growth, both spiritual and emotional. Welcome this opportunity, and you will view your relationships in a whole different manner. Instead of being fearful, you'll be excited. Instead of focusing on whether it will work out or not, you'll be focused on what it can bring to your life regardless of how long it will last. This is called living. Approaching a relationship, or anything else, out of fear is *not* living. It's more like expecting to die and wondering how it's going to happen.

Make a commitment to yourself to start living and enjoying everything life has to offer and learn to love again. Love yourself. Love your friends. Love life! And you will notice love coming back to you in different ways. It may be in the form of a lover, or the form of a better job offer or promotion. Whichever way it comes, it'll serve your life.

So, get ready to enjoy a new life. In order to change your life, you must first change your mind. Adopt a positive attitude and start expecting positive things to happen. It won't happen overnight, but just like a savings account, if you consistently deposit a little money at a time, before you know it, you will have accumulated a nice sum. Practice a little "positivity" every day and notice what happens in three months. Heck, you'll see the difference in a month!

Remember to stay positive, live authentically, know what you want, and never settle for being treated as less than what you're worth. Everything else will fall into place from there. Good luck and God bless!

978-0-595-41418-5
0-595-41418-4